The Sublime Landscape and Beyond

The Sublime Landscape and Beyond

An Artist's Retrospective and a Poet's Vision

poems by **Michael Baldwin**

paintings by **Johnny Bowen**

SHANTI ARTS PUBLISHING

BRUNSWICK, MAINE

The Sublime Landscape and Beyond

An Artist's Retrospective and a Poet's Vision

Published by Shanti Arts Publishing
Interior and cover design by Shanti Arts Designs

Shanti Arts LLC
193 Hillside Road
Brunswick, Maine 04011
shantiarts.com

Printed in the United States of America

ISBN: 978-1-956056-05-1 (softcover)

Library of Congress Control Number: 2021946717

Table of Contents

Paintings

Arkansas Landscapes

Texas Landscapes

Other Landscapes and Seascapes

Still Lifes

Introduction

This book is the result of a collaboration between two longtime friends who found they both appreciated each other's creative work: one a painter, the other a poet.

Johnny Bowen was offered a showing of his paintings at the Arts Center of the Ozarks, Springdale, Arkansas, in June 2009, recognizing him as one of the major painters of Arkansas. Michael Baldwin, an award-winning poet, had previously written several well-received poems for Bowen and his family for various occasions, so Bowen asked Baldwin to write poems for each of the paintings in the show. The project became a labor of love as Baldwin saw the high quality and inspired vision in Bowen's paintings. The show was a great success, both the paintings and the poems gaining many compliments. Since then, both individuals have gone on to garner significant respect and praise for their work.

Baldwin has continued to write poems related to Bowen's paintings and has produced two poetry books that included a few of Bowen's paintings. In 2020, Baldwin decided it was time to publish a book dedicated entirely to Bowen's art and Baldwin's poems. *The Sublime Landscape and Beyond* is the result of that collaboration. It is hoped that readers will appreciate the beauty of Bowen's artwork and enjoy Baldwin's poems, intended to enhance the experience of viewing the paintings.

In order to appreciate the background ideas and activities that figured in the making of this work, Bowen and Baldwin have provided notes at the end of the book on each painting and poem. These notes provide interesting background for how the paintings and poems came to be created.

The artists hope you enjoy *The Sublime Landscape and Beyond* and find in its paintings and poetry a sense of the awesome and sublime that they have experienced and tried to communicate through their work.

The Sublime Landscape

by Johnny Bowen

For most of my life, I assumed that sublime simply referred to something grand or exquisite. In fact, this is one of the definitions given in the dictionary, but it can also refer to something that inspires awe as a result of some elevated quality such as beauty or grandeur. When I began painting, at age fifty, I had some familiarity with the Hudson River School of artists, including Albert Bierstadt and Frederic Edwin Church. Their paintings aroused feelings in me similar to the feelings I experienced the first time I saw the Rocky Mountains. The depictions of grand vistas in the American West by these and other artists of that period aroused my senses of wonder and, yes, awe.

I also learned that the word sublime has had deeper, philosophical meanings. As understanding of the natural world increased (aided by the Copernican Revolution, Isaac Newton's discovery of apparent universal laws of physics, and the beginnings of modern geology and chemistry), the concept of the beautiful versus the mysterious began to occupy the minds of philosophers and theologians. Philosophy in the eighteenth and nineteenth centuries was not a separate endeavor from science and politics. During this Age of Enlightenment, all creation and man's activities on earth were thought to be interrelated; it was all a puzzle meant to be solved by rational thinking and experimentation.

This interest in and growing knowledge of the natural world affected the perception of landscape art during this period. While some landscapes were meant to be beautiful, other landscapes were meant to show the natural world in all its fierceness and wildness. The concept of the sublime took on a connotation of the feeling of awe bordering on fear as the viewer looked on the rugged, wild landscapes painted by Thomas Moran, Albert Bierstadt, Thomas Cole, and others.

In theology, this concept of sensing a force or power outside of one's self can be described as a terrifying mystery (*mysterium tremendum*) or as a fascinating mystery (*mysterium fascinans*). In his introduction to the book *Ansel Adams, Yosemite and the High Sierra*, John Szarkowski writes about Adams's description of his increased sense of perception in the Sierra Mountains:

> Adams is seeing the world from some condition of heightened awareness; perhaps he is experiencing the sublime, that condition so often spoken of in the nineteenth century and never satisfactorily defined, but which seems to have been a kind of holy terror, a happy kind of fear—an exaltation that came with the recognition of one's insignificance. As it concerned the natural world, the sublime was most often associated with immensity—with great spaces, cataracts, towering mountains, and the apprehension of enormous power.

I am not a philosopher, and I am certainly not qualified to explain the history of the word sublime. I do know, however, that when I look at the spiral arms of the Milky Way on a clear Ozark night and try to contemplate the incomprehensible vastness of the universe, I feel the *mysterium tremendum et fascinans* of that reality. And when I stand atop Hawksbill Crag, overlooking a mountain valley shaped by millions of years of geologic changes, I am experiencing the same feeling of awe that poets, philosophers, and artists have tried to describe for millennia. It is my aspiration to try to convey this feeling in some of my paintings.

Arkansas Landscapes

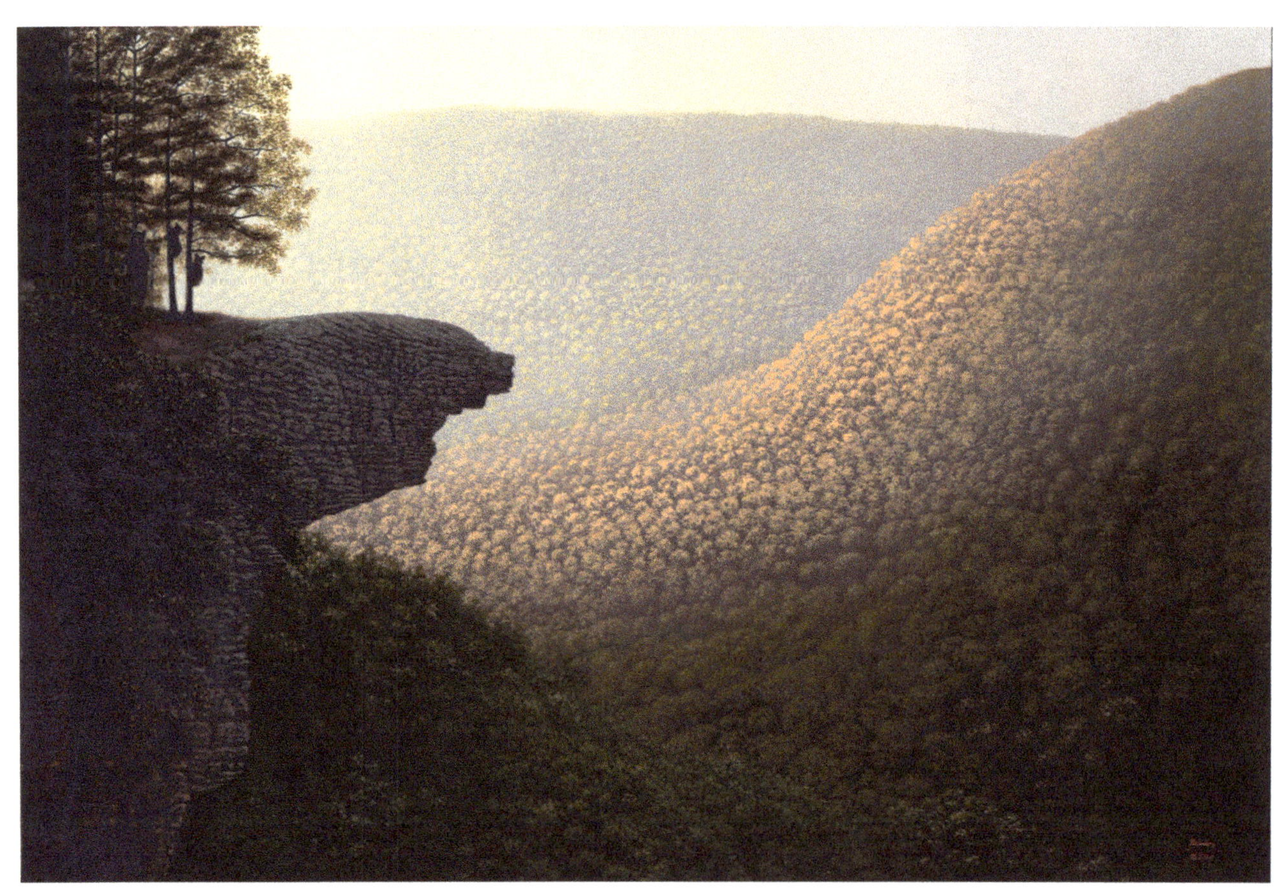

Dawn in the Wilderness (24 x 36)

*Mysterium Tremendum**

The huge outcropping of ancient,
eroded limestone known as Hawksbill Crag
leaps from the wooded mountainside
into the void above the valley
and cries out in awe and wonder
as it hangs over that vastness,
still grasping the mountain with
inward claws, while gasping
in astonishment, not at the beauty
of the vista, but with startled terror
and exhilaration in the immense
space of this million-year moment.
Does the sow bear sense
the vertiginous spirit of the scarp
as she guards her cubs upon the crag?
Can only the human mind
experience this exalting fall
toward the infinite, this soul-shock
of the sublime?

* *Mysterium Tremendum* (terrifying mystery):
the spiritual terror provoked by an
overpowering spiritual experience

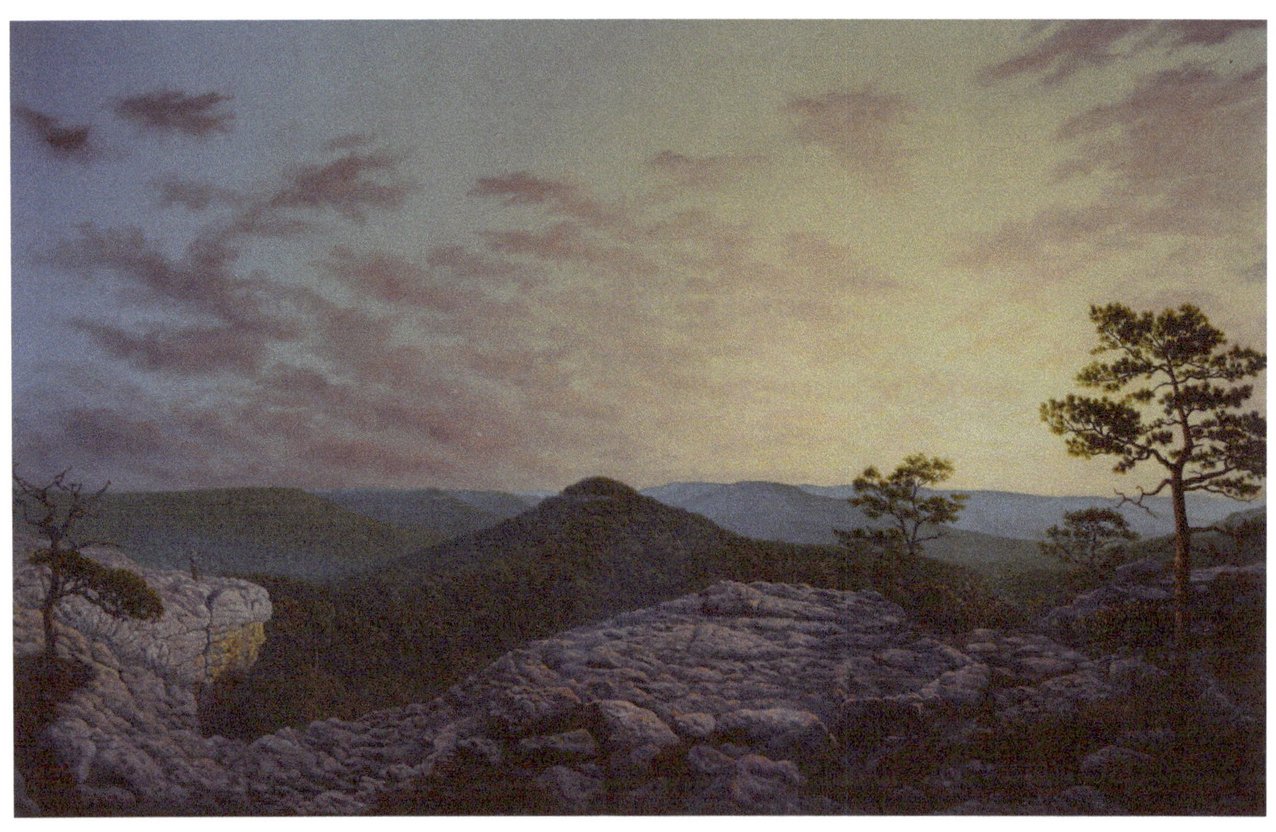

Summer Sunset at Sam's Throne (20 x 32)

Song for Sam's Throne

In the misty mountains of Arkansas,
sudden steep deepnesses
at the edge of the highway
can be both heart tightening
and soul exalting.
Motoring through Newton County,
we parked on a high stone ridge
to view Sam's Throne,
thrust up across the valley
like a defiant green fist.
And reading how Sam Davis,
in the 1820's, anguished at the loss
of his sister, kidnapped by Indians,
ascended that summit each day
for years to shout an angry
garbled gospel that mightily
annoyed his neighbors,
I backed my van to the verge
of that vastness, opened the doors,
with their built-in speakers,
intending to give the valley a hearing
of Vivaldi's gorgeous Gloria,
like a thousand love-crazed angels
rending the universe asunder with song.
But then I noticed the lone hiker resting
on his staff, admiring the sunset,
treasuring the tranquility of this place.
So I just leaned against the van and stared
across at Sam's Throne, illumined
by the golden glance of sunset.
Perhaps that was the hidden gold Sam
bragged about but no one ever found.
A red-shouldered hawk in a nearby tree
silently agreed and we shared for a moment
the serene magnificence of this mountain.

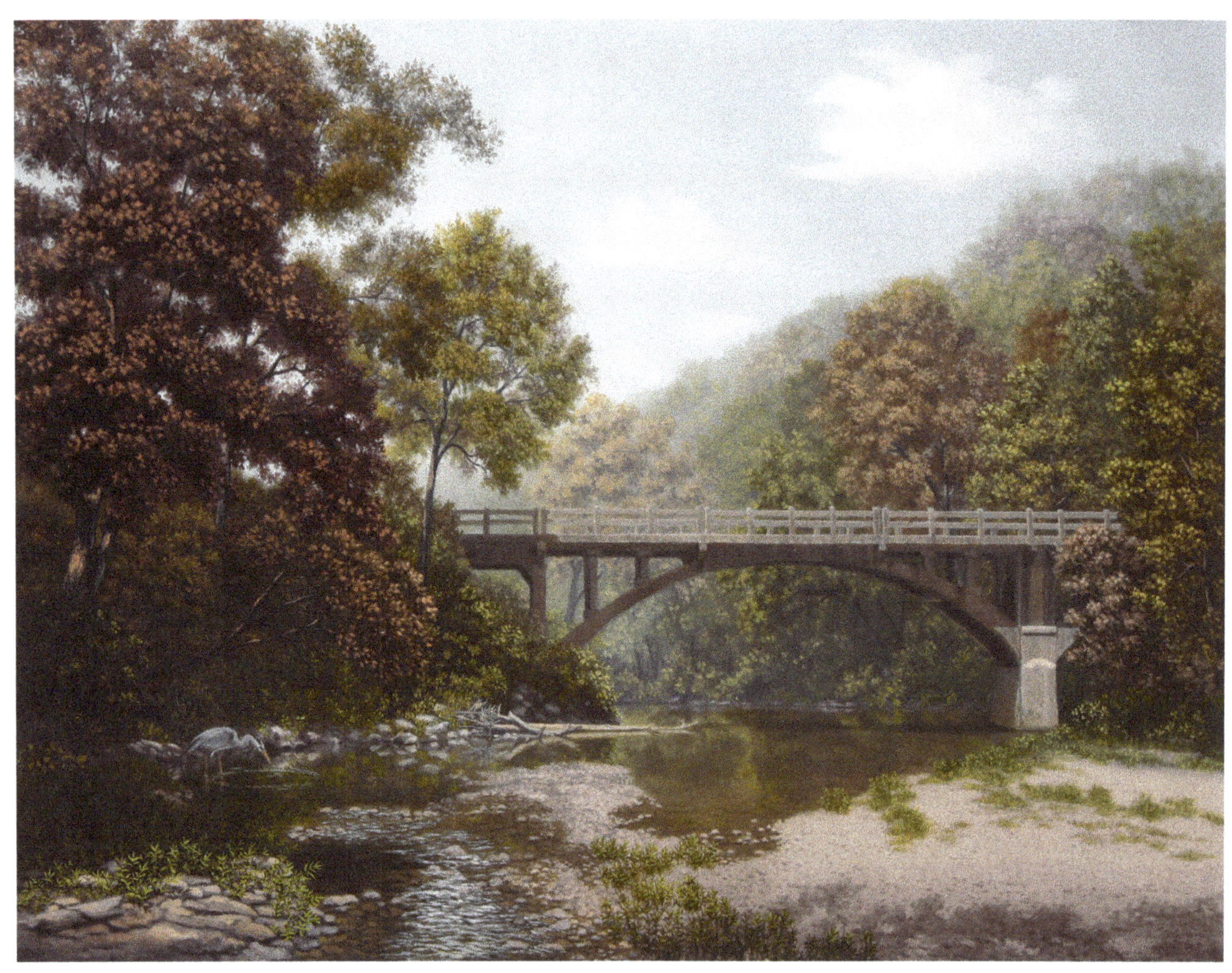

War Eagle Crossing (18 x 24)

Stillness at War Eagle Crossing

There is something in nature
that needs perfect stillness.
Yes, water loves movement,
loves to shimmer sunlight
in your eyes as it shivers
down a streamway.
Air, too, is enamored with
pushing clouds about the sky
and setting leaves atremble.
But nature finds some deep
satisfaction in the utter stillness
of a moment's eon,
as when a Great Blue Heron,
poised for a strike,
exactly imitates the arch
of the river's abandoned bridge
and all coalesces to utter calm
as nature meditates in perfect
stillness, as the universe itself
pauses
for an OM instant
between inhale
and exhale,
to contemplate its perfect beauty.

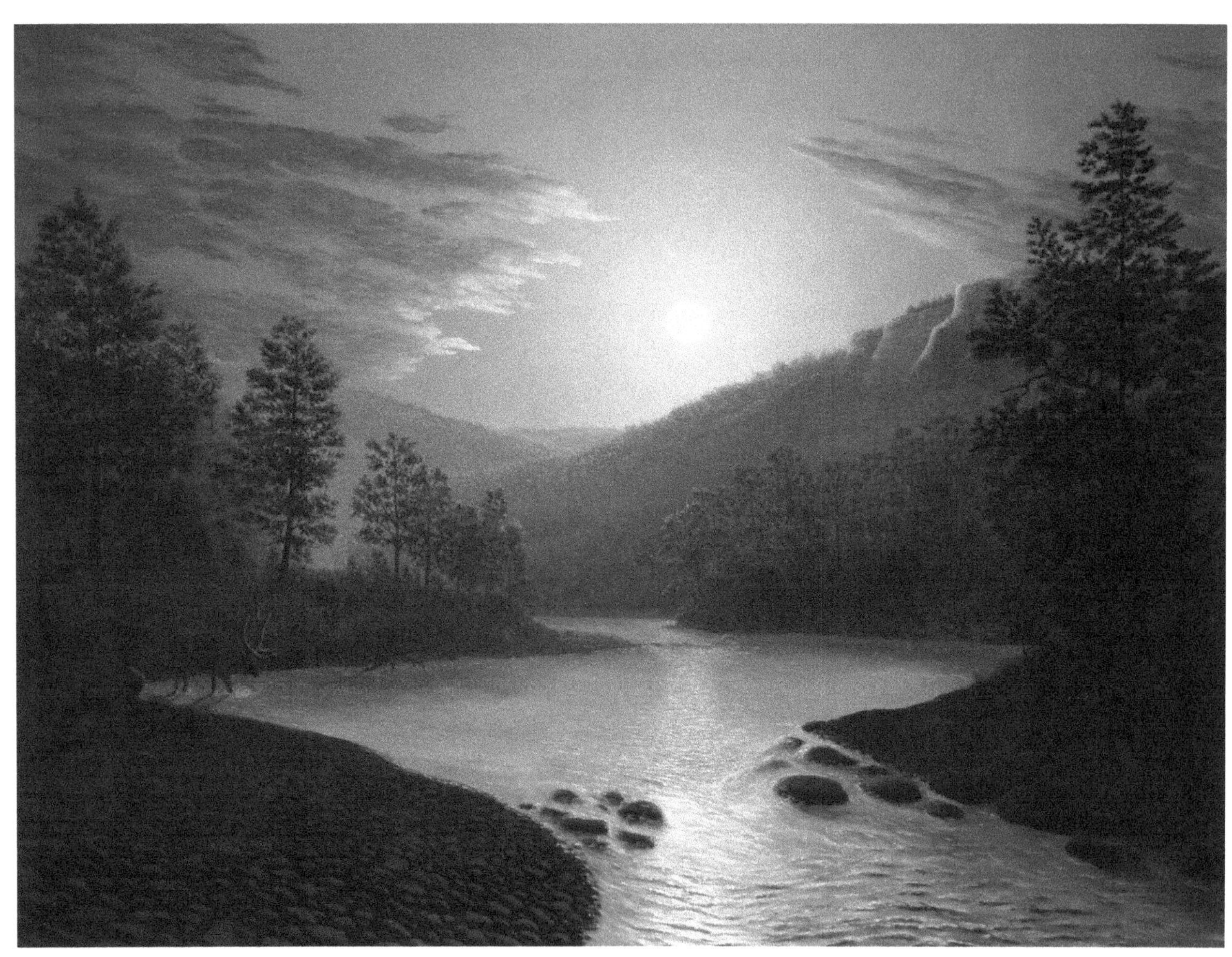

Moonlit Serenity (16 x 24)

Buffalo River Nocturne

Nature makes music by night.
Darkness engages our ears
and our imagination with
melodious murmurs,
symphonic susurrations of
water ripples rivering
among rocks, tree tongues
set singing by night breezes,
insects, frogs, and night birds
blending in concert.

But always it is the moon
that enchants the night,
gliding among glowing clouds,
casting such etheric luminance
upon the water that all beings
become imaginary, become
ghosts of themselves,
even our selves.

So, wading elk may be spirits
from an age before man,
manifesting when moonlight,
bent back into its own albedo
by moon's and water's mirrors,
becomes a sacred, timeless,
noctilucent, entranced
entrance for imaginings.

Thus the night mind
mothers our ancient children
and sings them lullaby.

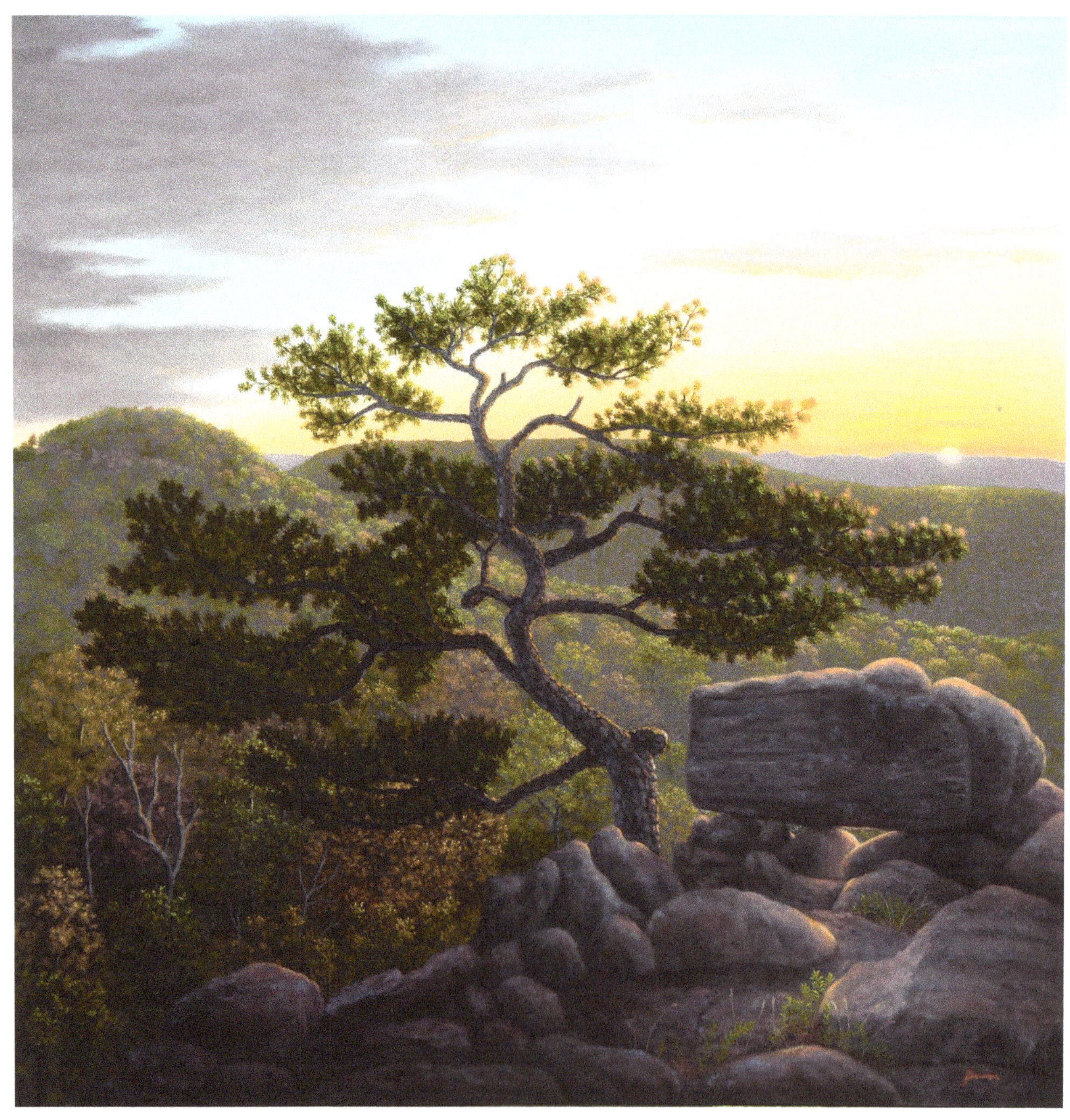

Ancient Sentinel (20 x 20)

Ancient Sentinel

An ancient Bristlecone Pine
twists into the emptiness
above this immense valley,
contorting as if in fear.
But that's just projection of
your own anxiety of the height,
as you lie, supine upon the smooth
precarious expanse of stone beside
the tree, trepidatious, expecting
any moment to hear the sliding scrape
of rock against rock, before you
careen into the yawning abyss
just inches beyond.
Yet you realize the tree has clung
this cliff hundreds of years,
perhaps conversed with the even
older boulder in their slow language
of wind scour, of rain pockings,
of roots clinging companionably,
witnessing on cold, clear nights,
star stories, writ in photon phosphors
upon sky's dome of hard darkness.
And thousands of sun comings,
each unique, spriting brightly
among far horizoned hills,
bringing warmth to the stone,
nourishment to the tree. Ah, now
you feel welcome and at home.

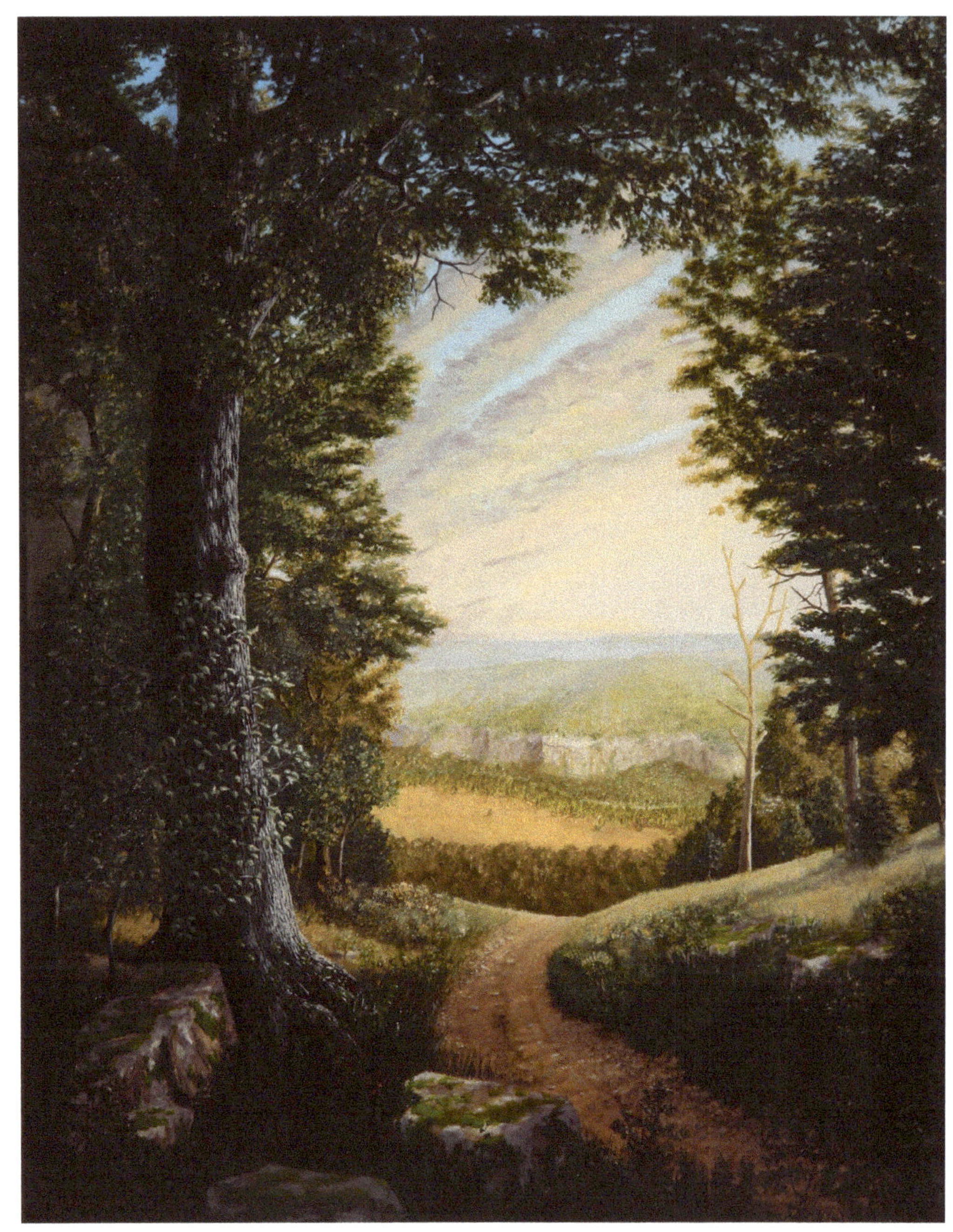

Ozark Memory (16 x 20)

The Journey

Trails were worn through wilderness
by migrating beasts and man,
since time immemorial.
Man evolved to wander,
following herds as hunter-gathers
for myriad millennia. So wander-lust
is the very marrow of our bones,
the plural branching pathways of our brains.
We still journey from unknown to unknown,
wandering aimlessly or aimed, mind-maimed,
questing a path through our mind's dark forest
into that golden, sunlit country
of fulfilled desire. Forgetting
that utopia means nowhere.
Who are we who obsessively search,
enduring hardships and humiliations,
for we really know not what?
Where are the beauty and wonder
we have lost in treading only
the well-trampled road?
We instinctively seek
an ever elusive something, some
where that is not here,
a perfect end to
an imperfect journey,
only to find, in the end,
just the journey itself.

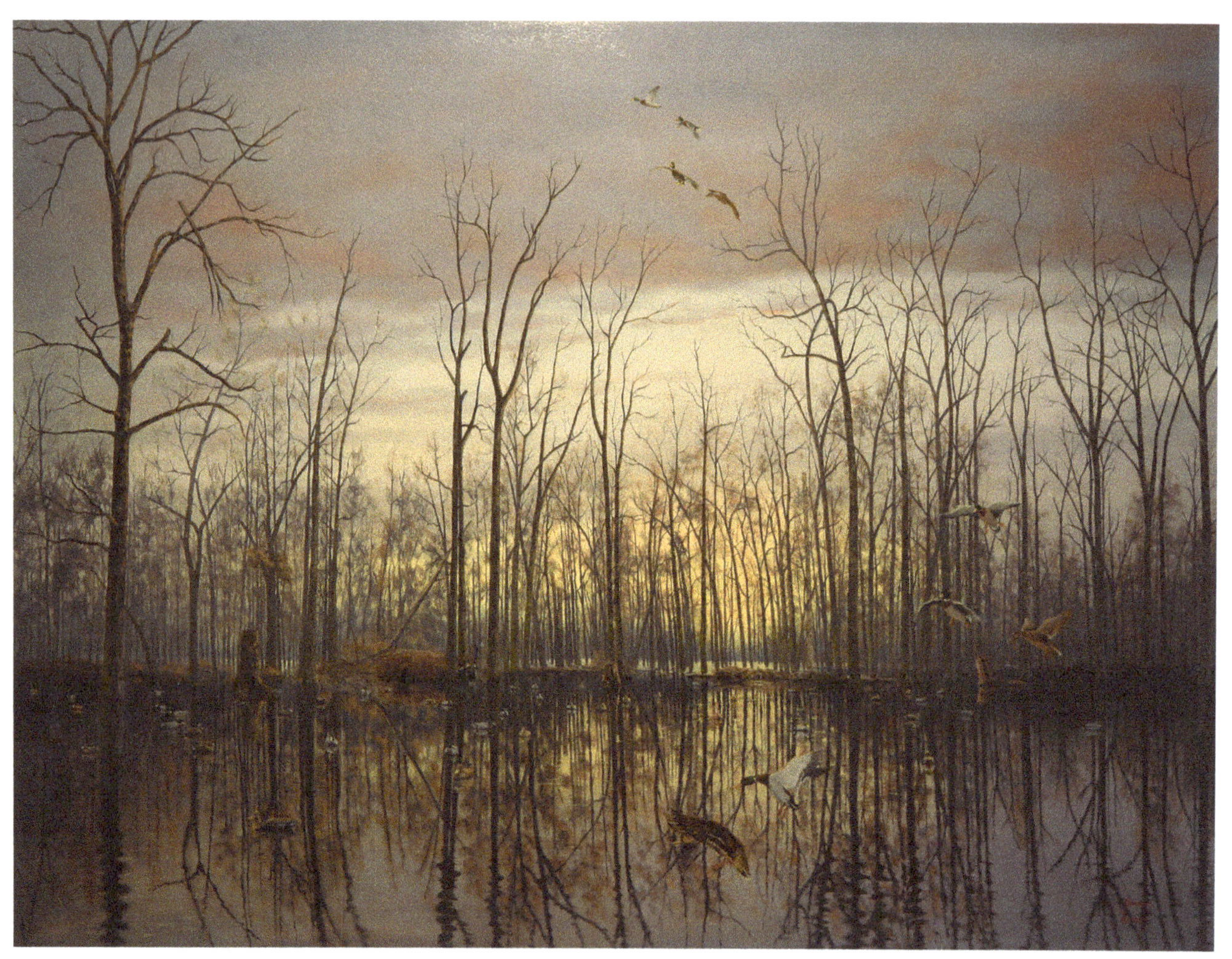

Gillett Farms Mallards (18 x 24)

On Golden Pond

How could a swamp, created by
flooding a lowland stand of timber,
drowning the trees in the process,
to create a killing pond for ducks,
be deemed beautiful?
Yet, when the air is overcast
with a turbid damp that oozes
into your bones, and, with that moist
density, refracts the dawning sunlight
into a diffuse, lambent, golden nimbus,
even the stark trees, stripped skeletal
by an ice storm, shivering naked
on the chill, glowing pond mirror,
instill an eldritch beauty that beckons
the ducks to descend, hens first,
then the emerald-headed drakes,
their braking feathers whistling,
until, just before touching water,
they sense the terrible
stillness of the decoys.

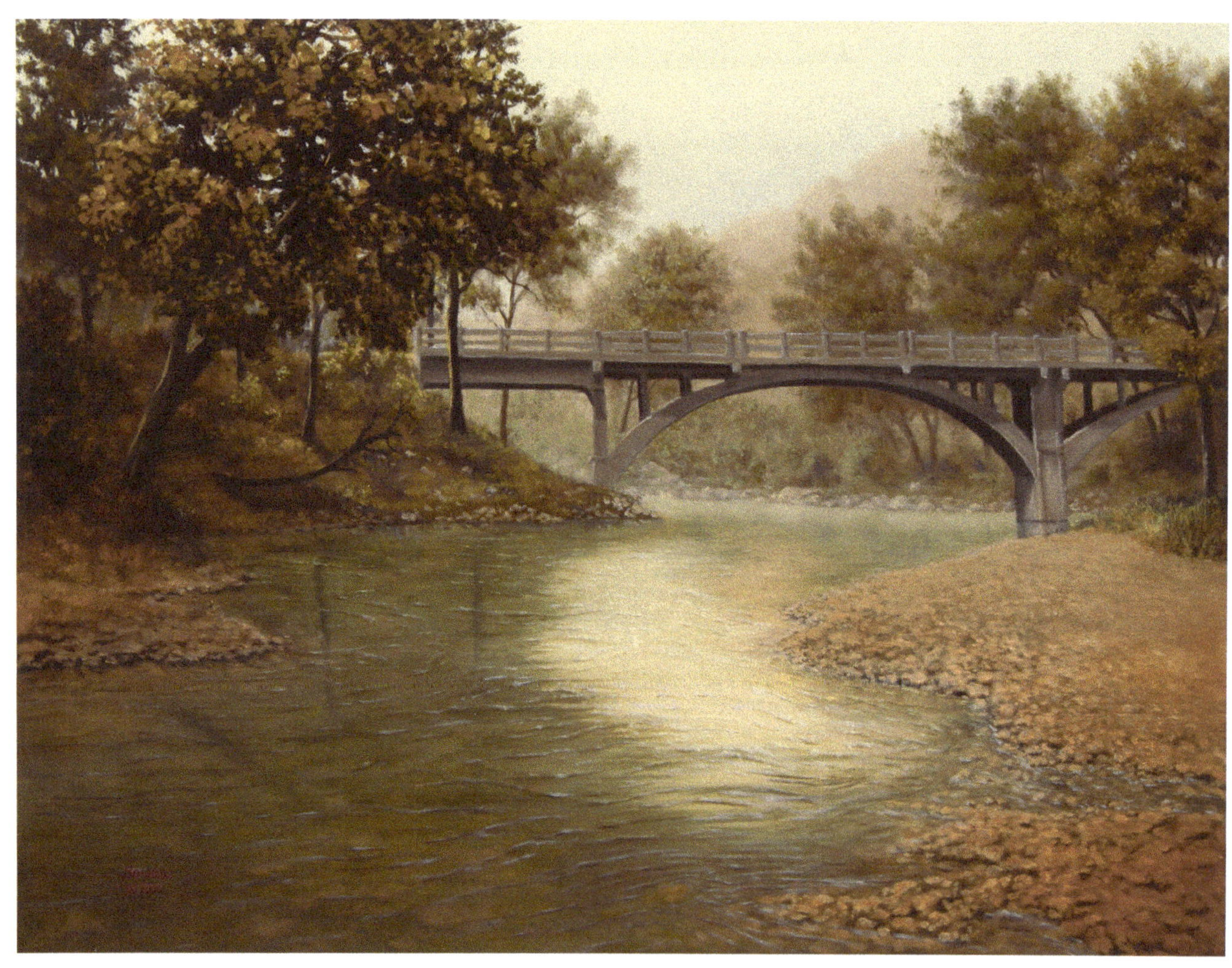

Peaceful Crossing (9 x 12)

Peace at Old Arkansas Bridge

As highways came to rule even the rural,
many old dirt roads were by-passed,
neglected, unneeded, except for access to
highways with a fast farewell.
If an old bridge residing on an old road
became too expensive to maintain,
not necessary to freeway travelers,
it was abandoned to slowly, gently rot,
to be forgot except perhaps by fisher folk,
adventurous children, lovers of the picturesque.
Such bridges quickly went to wild nature, became
a daylight sanctum for colonies of dozing bats,
a structure where swallows swath their mud nests,
sanctuary for wasps, spiders, lizards, snakes, all
those necessary critters among whom
we refuse to live in harmony.
This old bridge over War Eagle Creek shelters,
welcomes, all creatures, including us, if we
can but unthink ourselves a while.
Even unseen stones, dreaming deep within
the river's dancing mind, become
some integral gestalt with all that's human-seen,
as nature meditates, contemplates in its totality,
the peaceable kingdom She has created
for the human mind to appreciate, to emulate—
or to ignore in our ignorant worldly strivings.

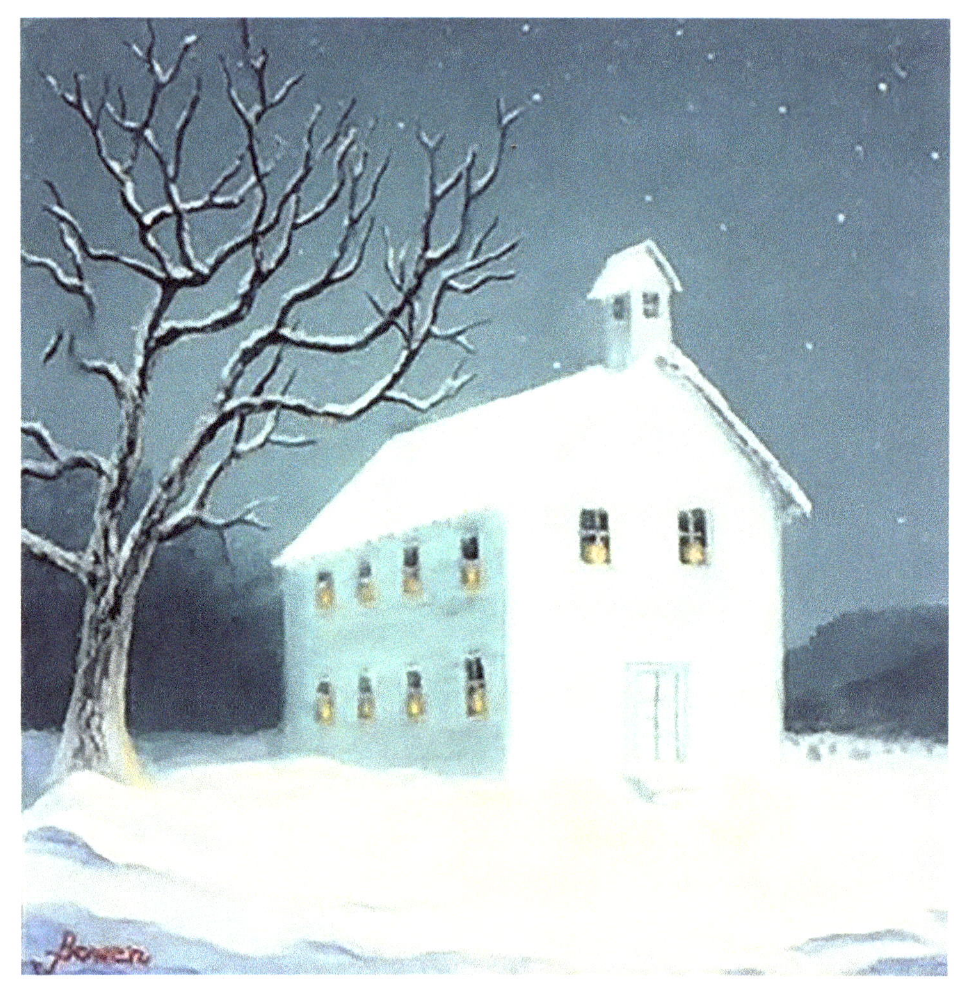

Silent Night in Boxley (5 x 5)

Silent Night in Boxley

Silent night,
silent white,
silent bright,
illumined beyond
windows' candlelight,
tree praying,
stars displaying,
silently arraying,
amid encroaching
darkness, around, above,
silent saying,
silent peace,
silent love.

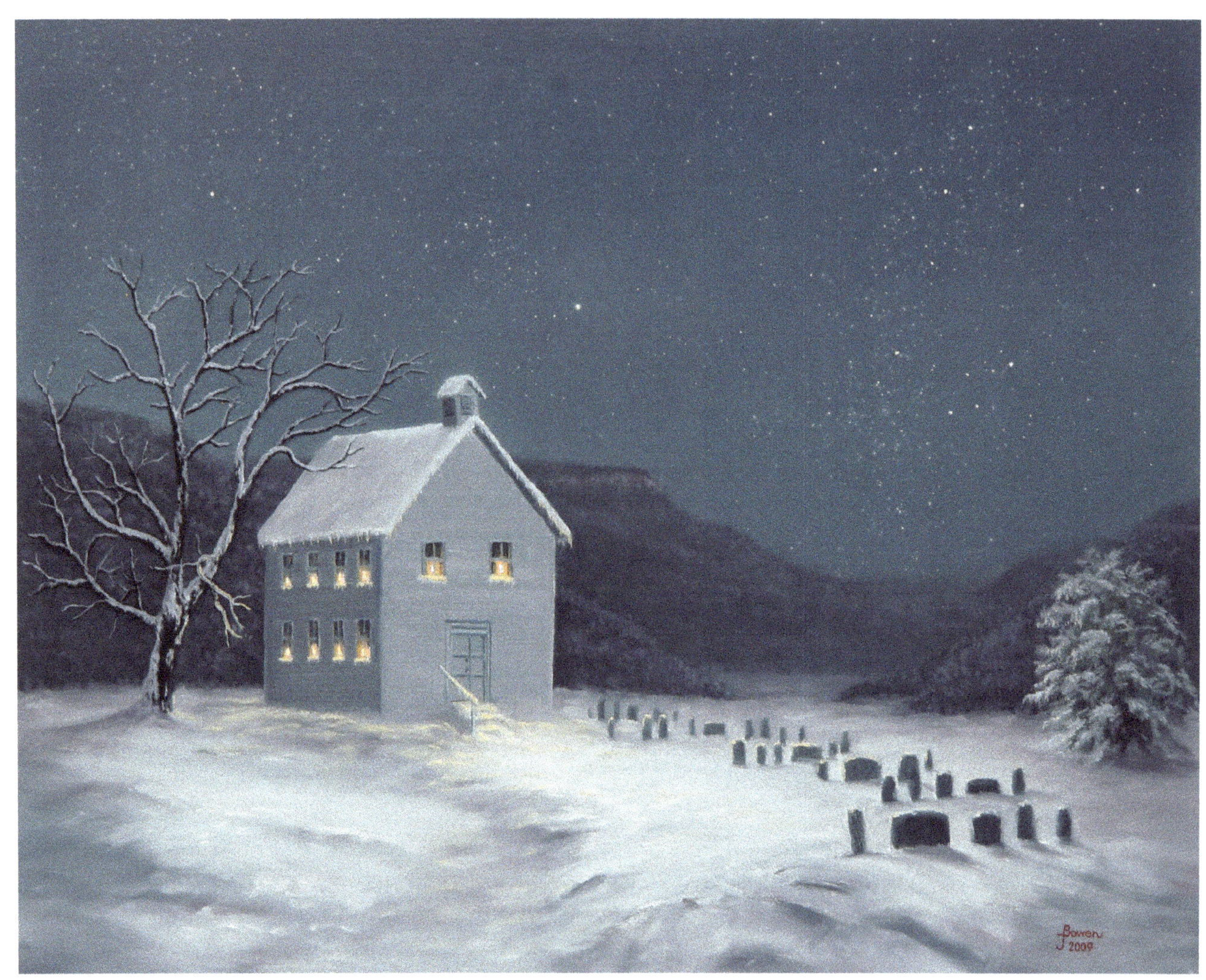

Eternal Lights (11 x 14)

Staring up the Stars

Crisp winter nights among mountains
are best for watching the stars.
Only an empty, snow-blown cemetery
can make their viewing even better.
Lean against a century-old gravestone
and let the cold seek your bones
as your eye finds the Northern Cross
bright above the western hills.
Let your mind fall into the stars.
Allow your awareness to wander
the hypnotic vastness of the universe
until you are immersed in the stars'
imaginings, sharing their cosmic musings.
Stars died to become human.
Native Americans believe we die
to become stars.
Mountains and trees have always
contemplated the stars.
It is the beginning of wisdom.

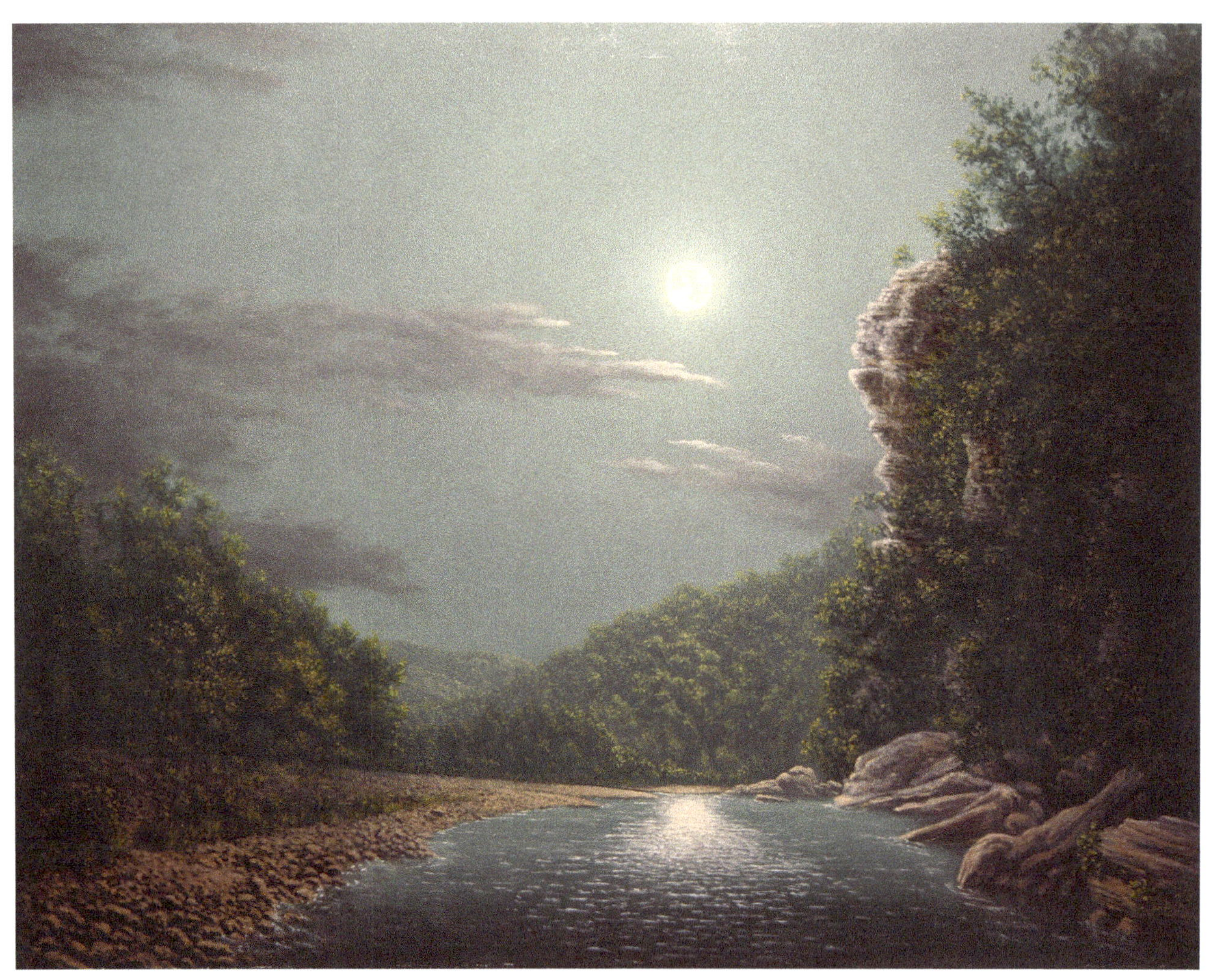

Steel Creek Sonata (11 x 14)

Steel Creek Sonata

The full moon feels afire
in the night sky, on the water,
having torn its veiling clouds,
now blares light against bare
sky like a silver trumpet
so fierce the night creatures
have fled to darker regions,
insects ceased their seridulations,
bushed birds bend into their feathers.
The granite cliff face mounting beside
the creek gapes at the hot moon
with mesmered awe.
All is soundless save the murmur
of the stream as it rides the scintillant
moon-path into infinity,
into this furious serenity.

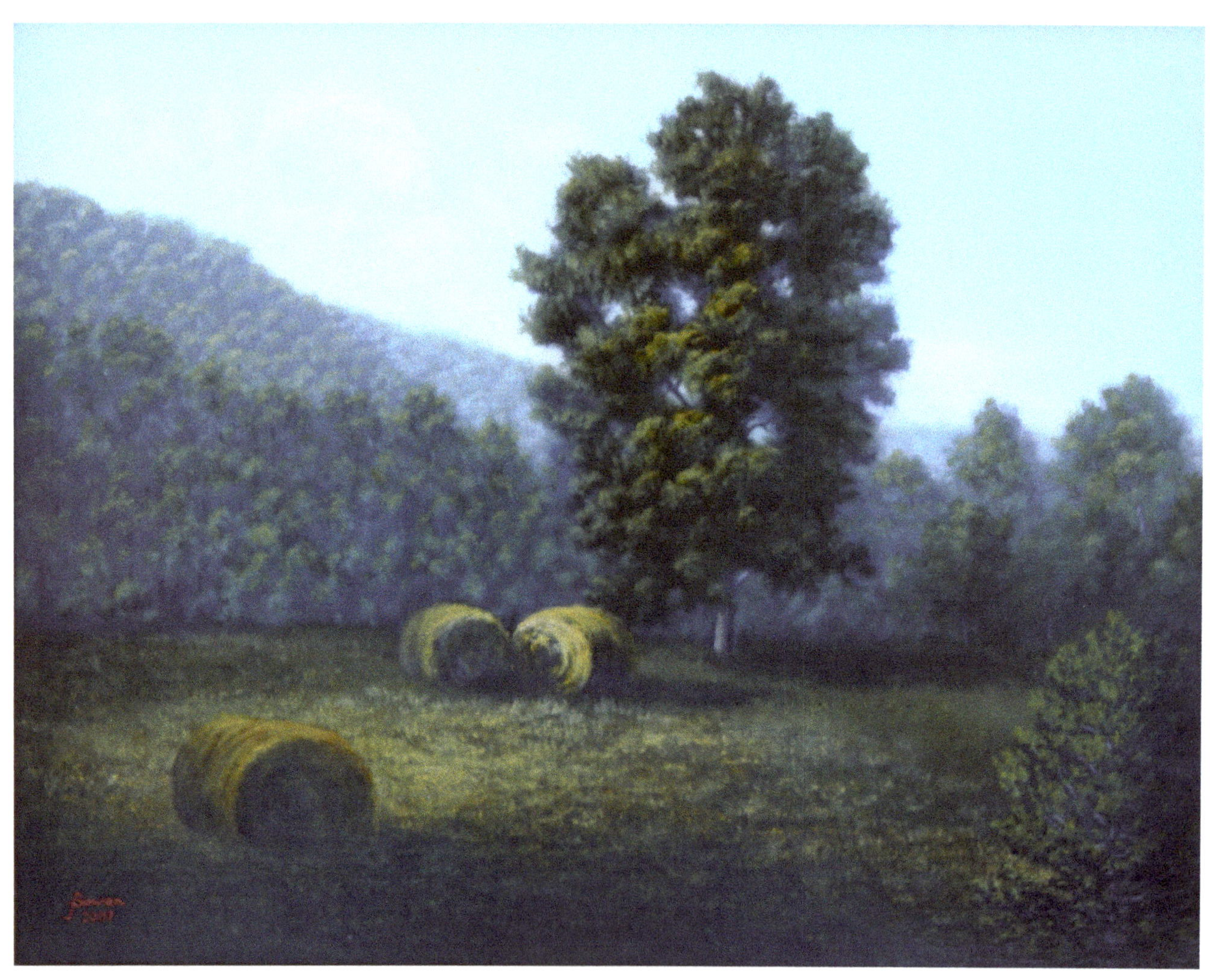

Hay Bales along the West Fork (10 x 13)

Abandoned Hay Bales

In the onslaught of evening
a lone majestic sycamore
rises birdless over a machine-
mown meadow inhabited by
three cylindered hay bales.
Trees crowd claustrophobically
upon the hills behind and around,
like spectators eager for action at
a football game or public spectacle.
Indeed, the hay bales might be actors
in some tragic play or opera: lovers
rendezvous, kiss, conspire in whispers,
while the villain skulks, stage left,
about to deliver his spiteful soliloquy.
Glowing in the gathering gloom,
these three seem freighted with
significance beyond the simple tableau
they present: a suggestion of lostness,
an intimation of abandonment, even
an evocation of emptiness of being,
perhaps the only remaining vestige
of a self-abandoned humanity.

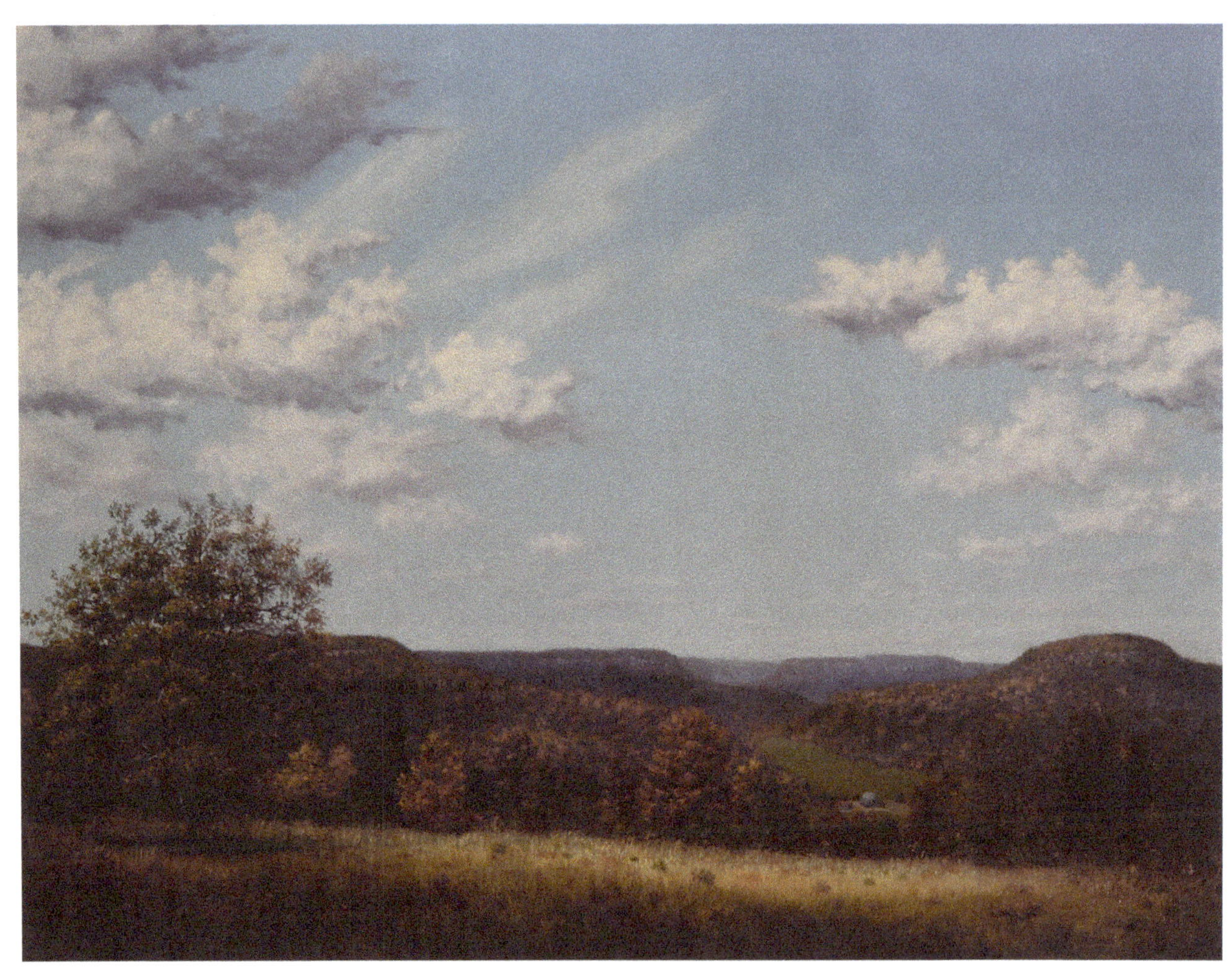

View of Boxley Valley (12 x 16)

View of Boxley Valley

Tramping aimless among these
verdant, cloud-shadowed hills,
just lazing after a sun shaft
as it glides along, urging my
attention to a flock of Firewheel,
interrupted by random up-thrusts
of slender snowy Crownbeard,
flushes of dainty mauve Elephantfoot,
then illumines a humble Hackberry,
setting it aglow with covert significance,
so the Hermit Thrush, hidden among
its foliage is stirred to offer
up a yearning tenor declamation,
a plaintive groan of languid lostness.
Then silence as the sunbeam slides
down the hill, toward the far white
church with its attendant cemetery.
I'll remain up here amid the flowers,
watch the sunray wind its way,
and hope the thrush will sing again.

Texas Landscapes

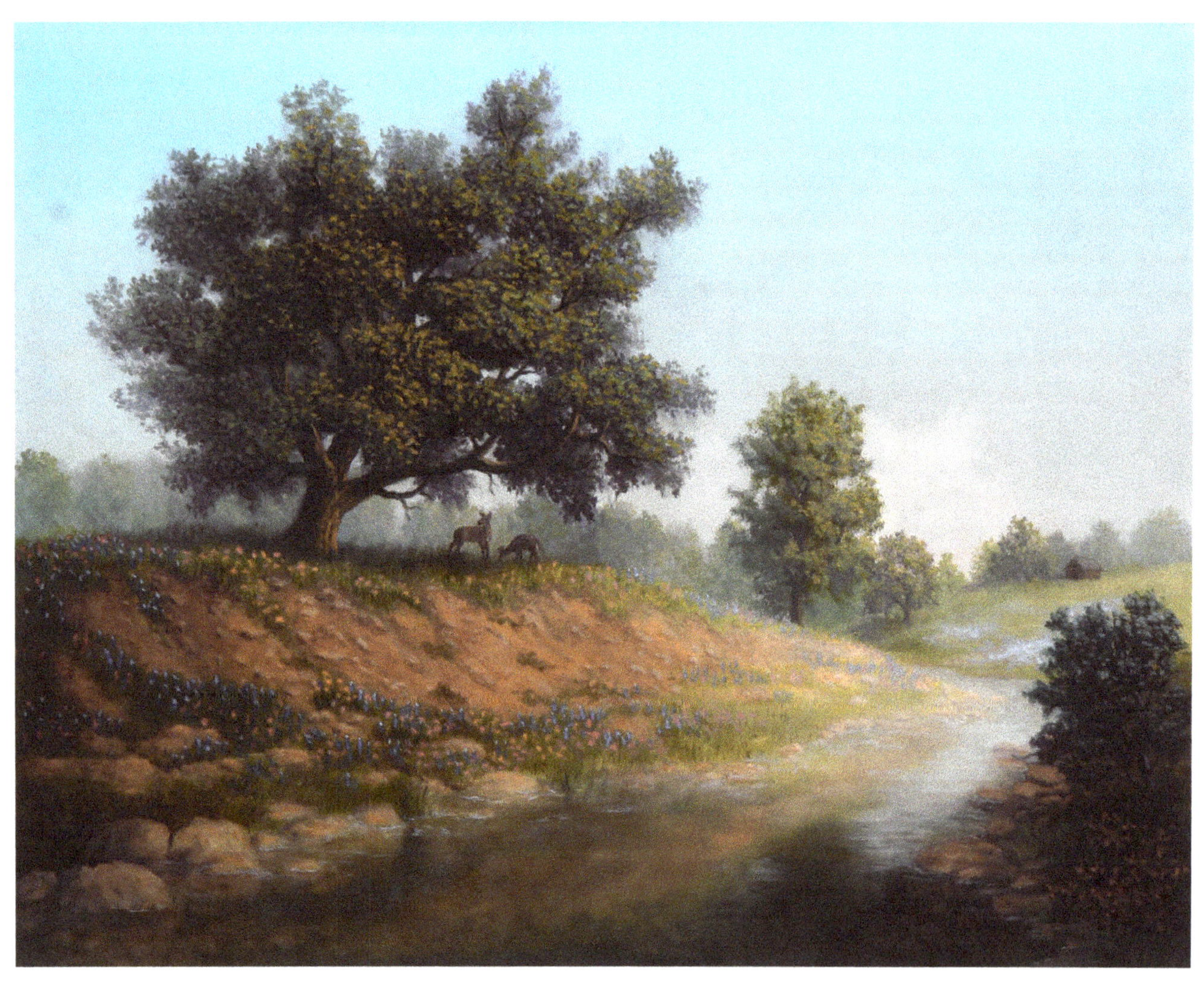

The Old Fishing Hole (11 x 14)

Speak, Water

The stream slides sinuously
along, always seeking the easy
way, but taking its time, enjoying
the panorama around each bend,
a blind old abandoned barn,
a troop of white helmeted Bluebonnets,
charging down the hill like cavalry,
a lonely oak leaning, eager to converse
with the voluble wandering water,
to learn what gossip the stream may
murmur of as it slows its flow
to relate its adventures for its
immobile arboreal friend.
The roving raconteur speaks
with fish flashes, with glistening
ripples, with stone whispers, with
plashing chatter of sun scatter.
The deer hear and understand.
Why are only we so deaf
to water wisdom?

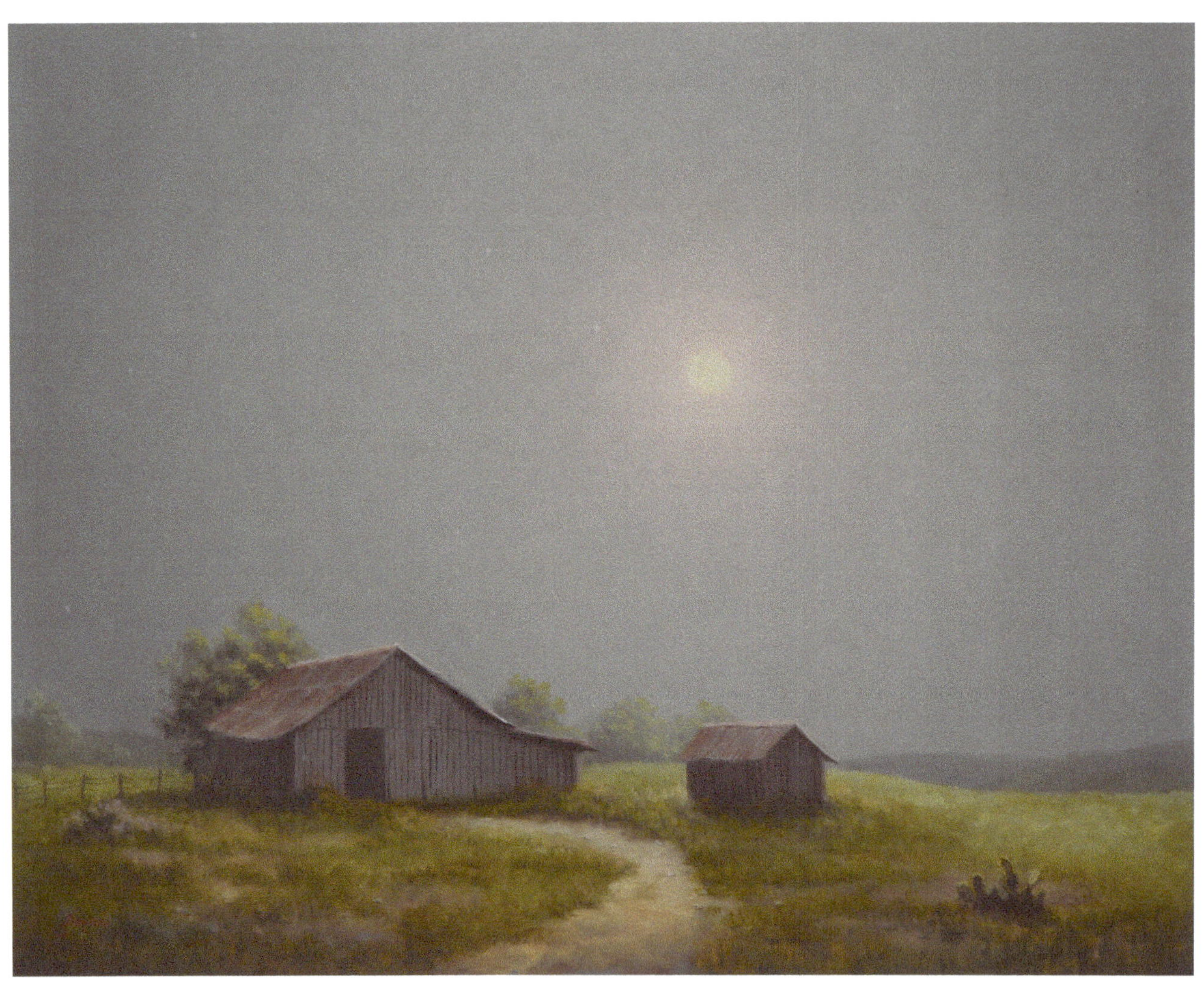

Gonna Be a Hot One (11 x 14)

Gonna Be a Hot One

Many a Texas ranch has a dilapidated
barn with corrugated iron roof that,
even though the day's barely begun,
already shimmers with heat waves
and groans complaintively as the rust
hots up, waking the red wasps nesting
in its rafters to buzz out and patrol their
harsh domain of Goat-Head, Bull-Nettle,
Purple Thistle, and grotesque green
Osage Oranges (uneaten since
the Giant Ground Sloth went extinct
twenty millennia ago), fresh fallen
from the Bois D'arcs along the fence line,
where only Prickly Pear actually revel
in the heat, blooming extravagantly
for a few desultory bees. Yes,
it's gonna be a hot one!

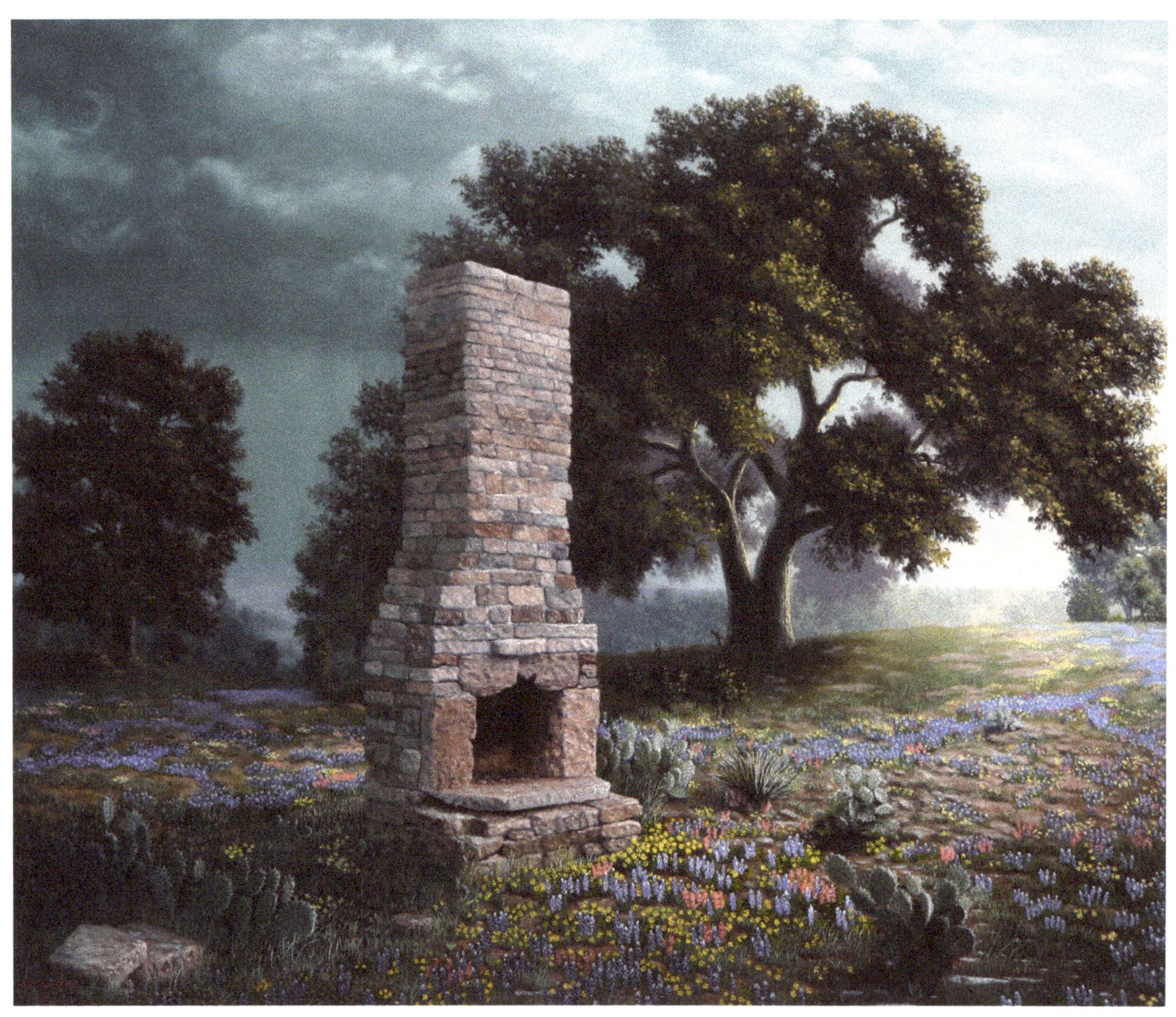

Spring Tonic (15 x 18)

Wildflower Witness

A mild, wet winter caressed
the earth and spilled
the Texas hills with flowers.
Firewheels whirl,
set blazing crazily
by sun shafts reclaiming
fresh-washed prairie
from a wandering thunderhead.
Coneflowers,
in ardent yellow,
mock Coronado's El Dorado.
Prickly Pear
save their blooms for summer,
but Bluebonnets
in proud profusion,
like a convocation
of Daughters of the Texas Revolution,
gather reverently around the ruin,
a granite pioneer hearth
forgotten by all but
a pair of hoary oaks,
and spend themselves in beauty
for this itinerant witness.

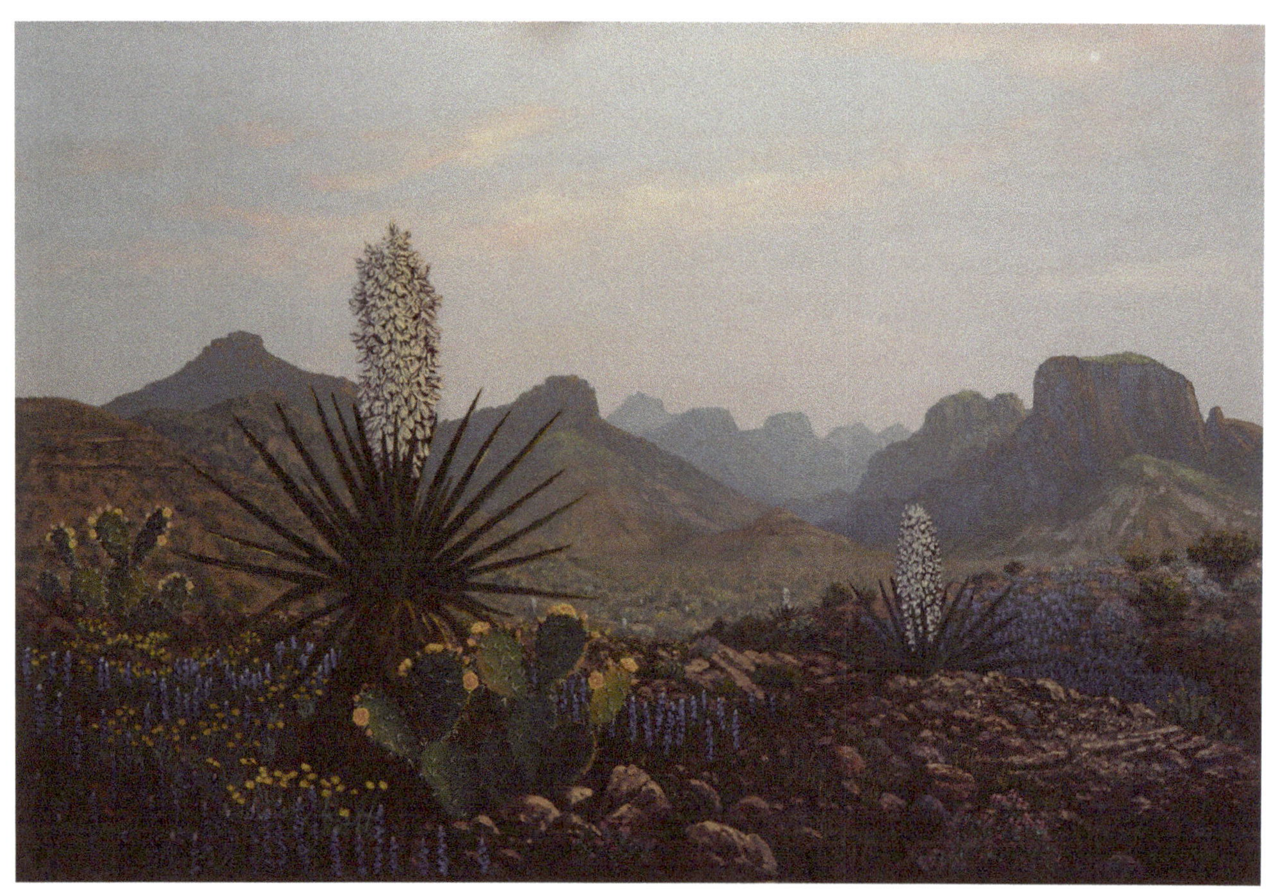

Chisos Splendor (24 x 36)

Chisos Splendor

We call them Adam's needle,
Giant Dagger, Spanish Bayonet,
and simply Yucca (its Indian name).
The species inhabiting Texas' Chisos
Mountains are particularly
formidable in this country so
arid and sun-battered.

Among these far mountains
and mesas, boulders and buttes,
Yucca give a thrusting brutal beauty
to a vista of thirsty distance.
In this ecology of bleak fecundity,
Yucca, Big Bend Bluebonnets,
Desert Marigolds, and Purple Sage
compete not for sunlight, but for water.
So Yucca send tap roots down
hundreds of feet for moisture,
then guard it with sharpness.

In summer, thousands of white flower
bells attract thousands of white moths
that couple the Yucca and bed their eggs
in balls of golden pollen to hatch within
the Yucca's seed pods; a marriage of
mutual necessity between insect and plant;
a mystery and a wonder.

If we could view this scene with God's eye,
we would see the energy of light
becoming the energy of life
in a vast complexity of harmony in diversity,
of extravagance in extremity,
of grace in grim circumstance—
Art is God's eye,
dauntless as yucca's dagger.

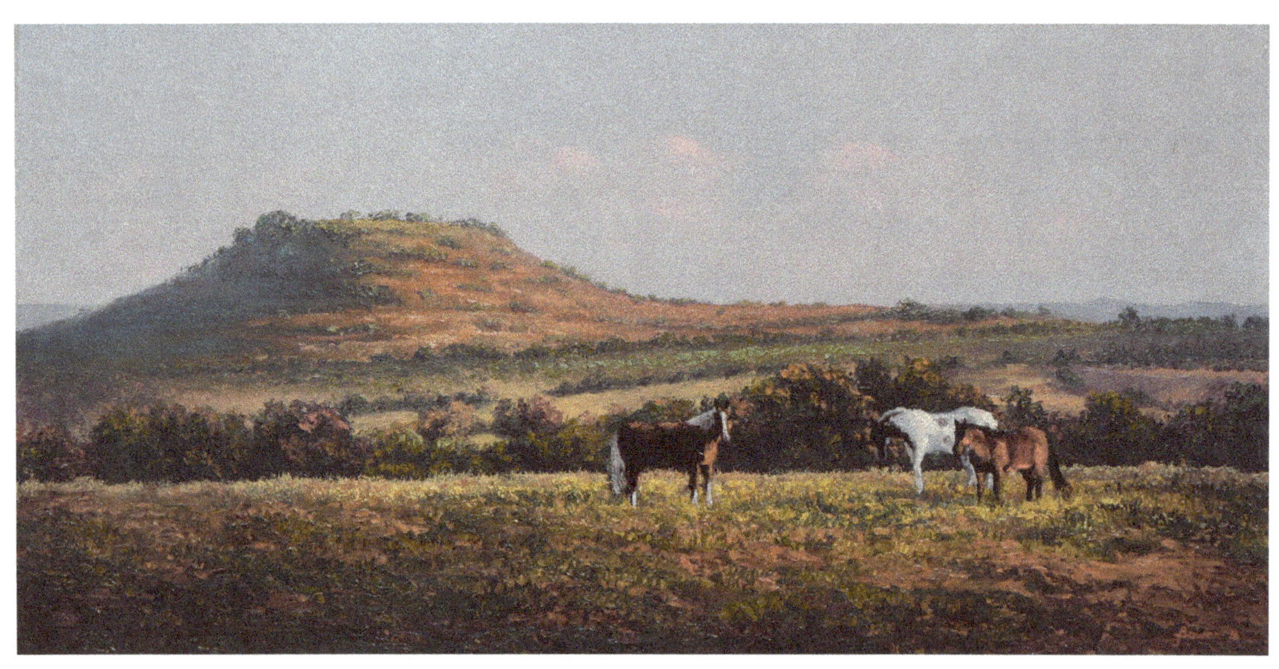

Texas Tranquility (12 x 24)

Mustangs

A mere 100,000 years ago, wild horses, *Equus ferus*, were native and numerous in North America, but they went extinct about 10,000 years ago, due, they say, to the end of the last ice age, or, perhaps, predation by Siberian nomads who wandered into a continent devoid of other human inhabitants. I'd like to think it wasn't Native Americans that killed off those horses, since they would have been too valuable for exploring, hunting, and warring.

Iberian horses played a major role in the Spanish conquest of Mexico in the 1500's. But when some became *mesteño*, strayed livestock, they quickly reverted to feral animals, adapted well to the vast Southwestern prairies, and multiplied prodigiously to become mustangs, mounts for *vaqueros*, cowboys, soldiers, and, indeed, became the salvation of Native Americans for 300 halcyon years, who were then able to harrow and hallow the buffalo herds from Texas to the far Dakotas. Mustangs transformed the Comanche, Apache, Kiowa, Cheyenne, Pawnee, and Sioux from powerless pedestrians into the mystic warriors of the plains, the greatest horsemen the world has known, and for whom horses became their medium of exchange, their means of livelihood, the center of their art and culture.

And, for Whites, mustangs made possible the adventuring, soldiering, and ranching that conquered the western continent. Now the prairie has become fenced pastures, furrowed fields, and cedar breaks. Pickups have replaced horses as the primary beast of burden. But the hills and prairies and the horses remain, perhaps dimly remembering in boulders and bones when the great West was horse country and when mustangs in their thousands, flowed across the prairies in flamboyantly colored rivers of flesh, exuberant in their freedom and magnificent in their perfect embodiment of those wilder, more wondrous times.

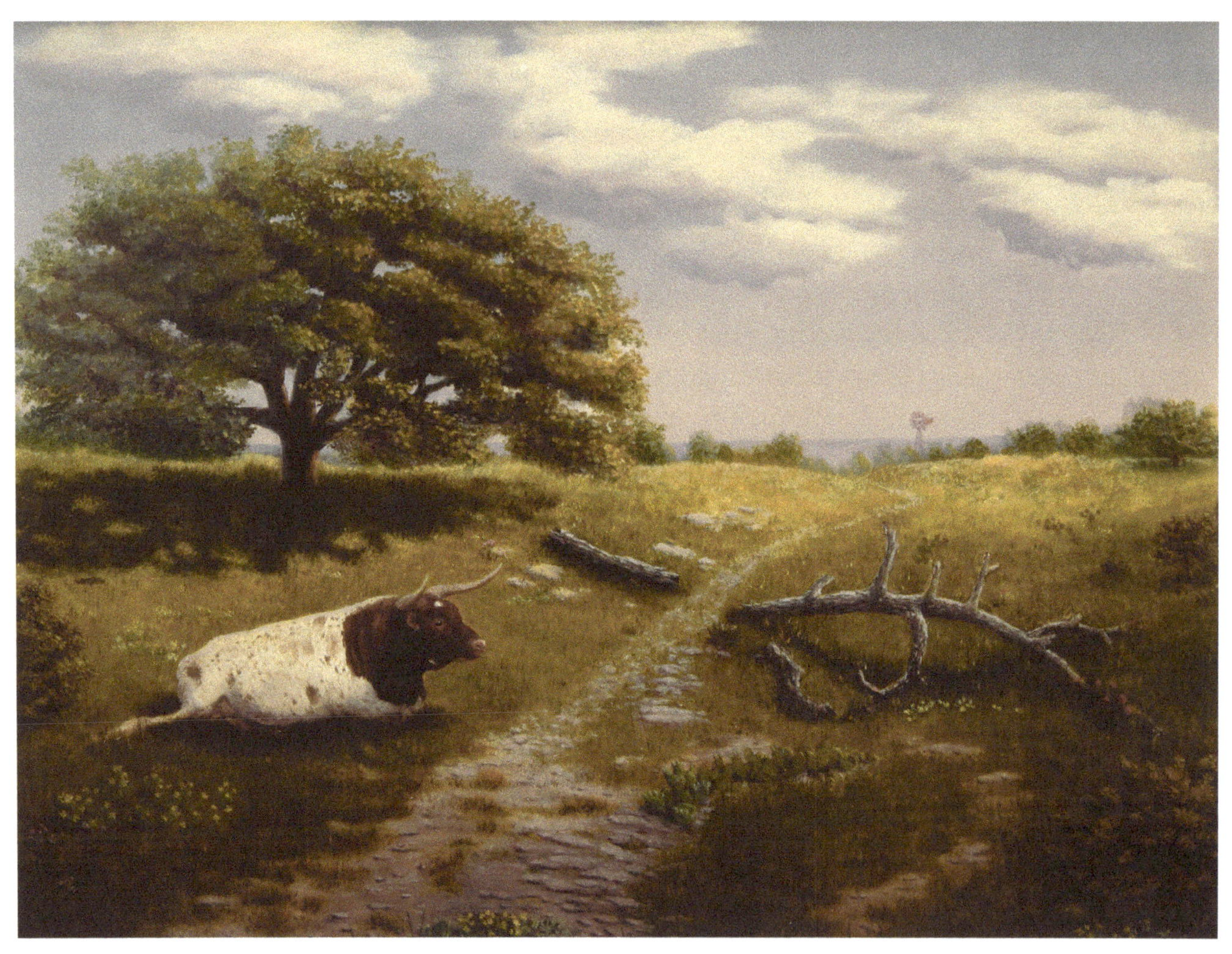

Johnny's Spot (12 x 16)

Pastoral Pastiche

Hot noon, cloud strewn;
oak shadows, dark echoes;
leaf laden, hawk hidden;
cow-pie plop, fertilizer flop;
high grass hiding, rabbit or coyote;
trail trampled, coming and going;
branch broken, almost antler;
mud puddled, rocks runneled;
Prickly Pears, conga chorus;
saffron Tickseed, crowd proudly;
uphill windmill, ungreasedly creaking;
brindled bull, friendly old fellow.

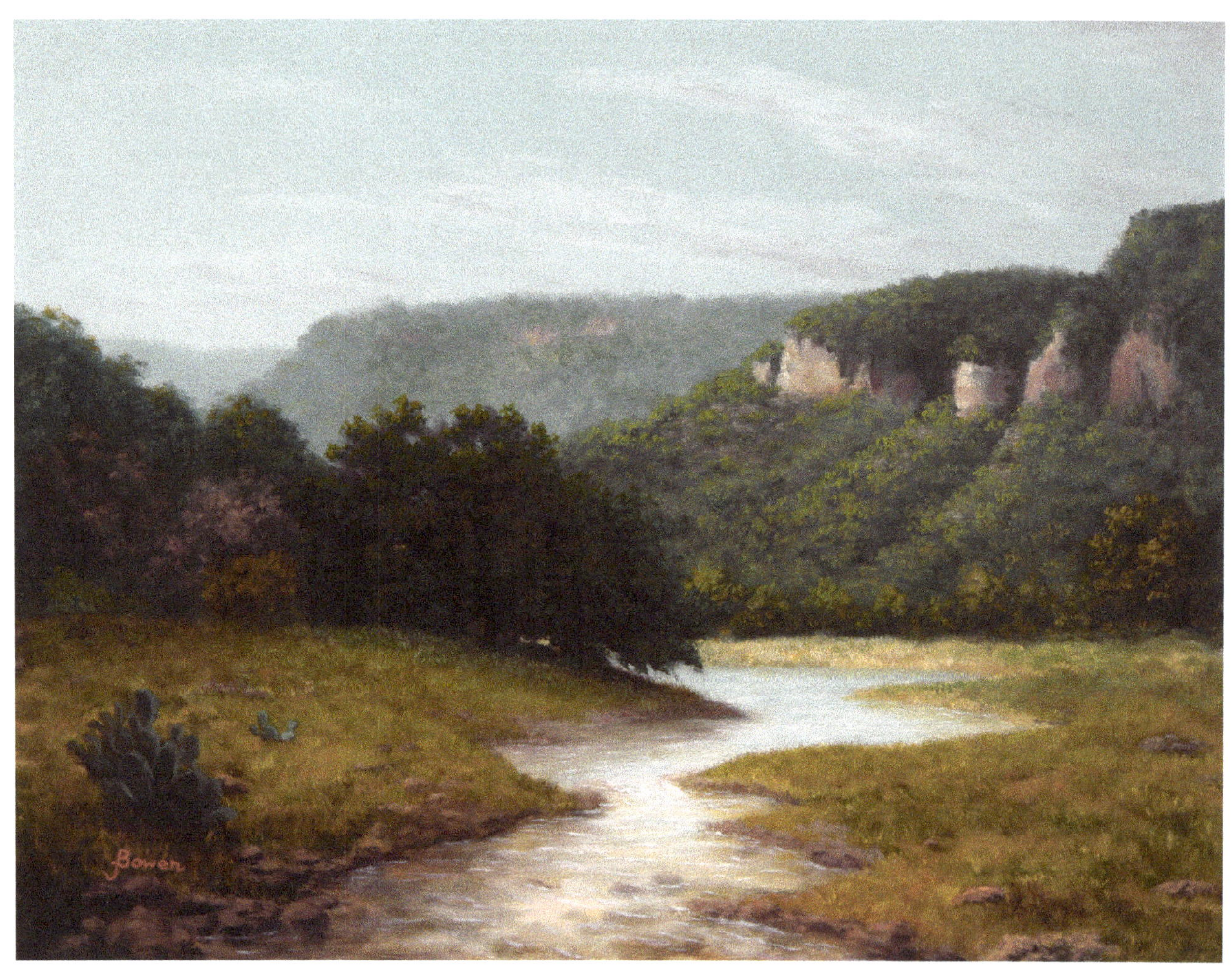

Utopia, Texas (9 x 12)

Utopia, Texas

Faces of bare limestone cliffs,
almost emulating Mt. Rushmore,
but clothed below in greenery,
overlook a zig zag stream
splashing through grassy pasture
of Prickly Pear and Indian Paintbrush.
This could well be a utopia,
both a "good place" and "no place,"
Sir Thomas Moore's little joke on
the title of his 1516 political satire.
Before it became Utopia in 1884, it
was idyllically beautiful, but had been
contended over by Spaniards, Indians,
and Anglos for a hundred years of
raids, massacres, attempts to settle
or exploit the land with blood and sweat,
much as with the rest of Texas.
For now it retains that natural beauty
which we have coveted and sought out
for hundreds of thousands of years, since
humans first became bipedal on the veldts
of Africa that must have looked much like
this particular Utopia.

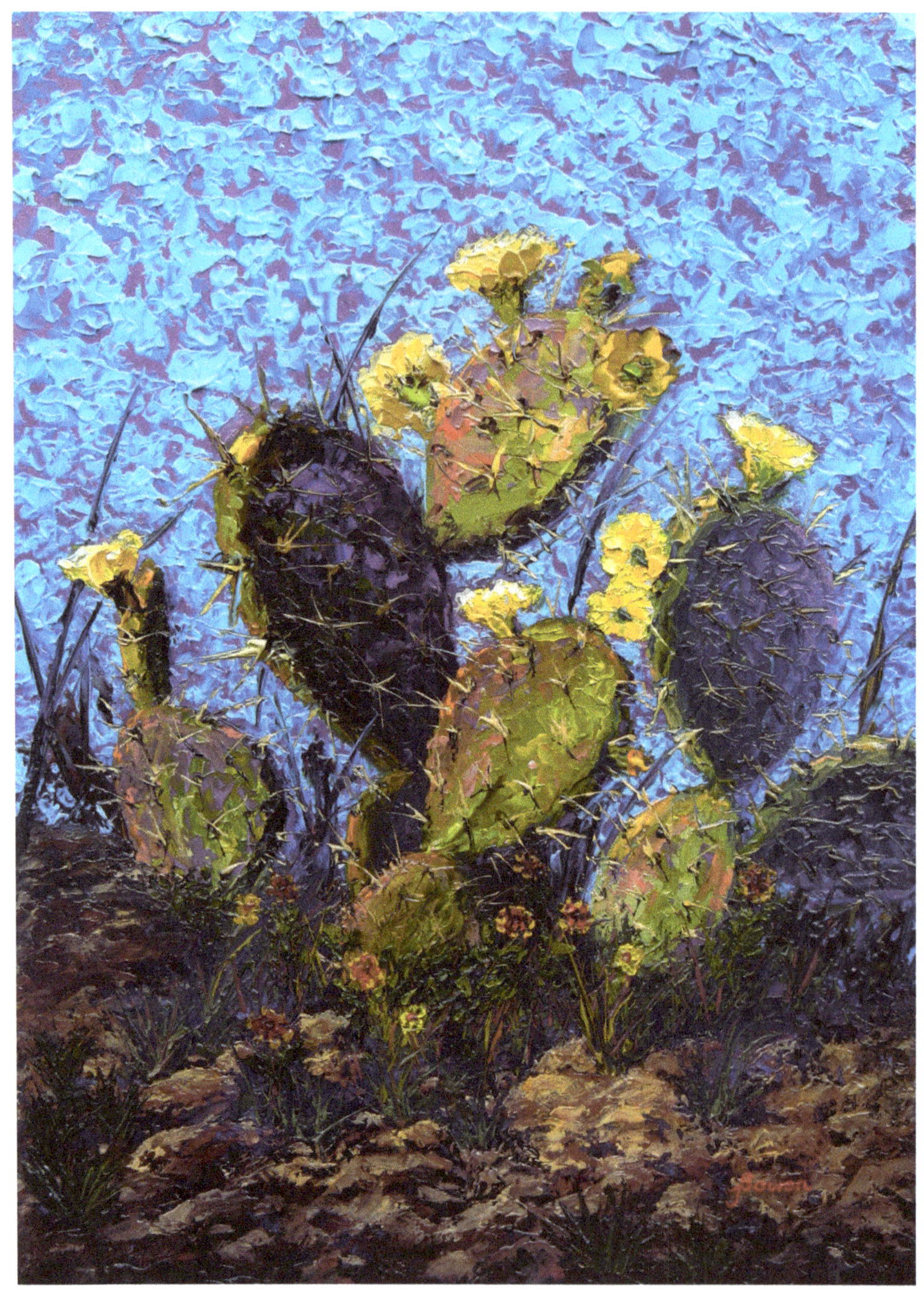

Prickly Pears (9 x 12)

Llano Estacado

Why write about blankness?
The "Palisaded Plains" Coronado called them.
But when he reached the top of this tableland,
he saw no landmarks to navigate by,
no trees or brush or boulders;
too high to see horizon.
It was an utter emptiness to desolate the soul.
More recent travelers say it is 85 percent sky.
This high desert became the last refuge
of Comanches pursued by foolhardy cavalry
into this harsh, thirsty emptiness.
Unknowing, they rode over the largest
underground lake in the world: the *Ogallala*,
laid down by glaciers two million years ago,
and hidden until deep wells could be drilled
through the hard cap rock to claim these plains
for cotton farms and Baptist churches.
Yucca knew there was water here.
Only it could send taproots down
hundreds of feet to sip that ancient water.
Perhaps the stumps of yucca were
what caused some to translate *Estacado*
as the "staked" plains, since these were
the only markers on the otherwise featureless prairie.
When the *Ogallala* is gone
(drunk dry for desiccated dollars),
the *Llano* will again be vacant of life.
Double empty; even the Yucca will vanish.
Desocupado, vacio, vacante.
Who will care to rename it?

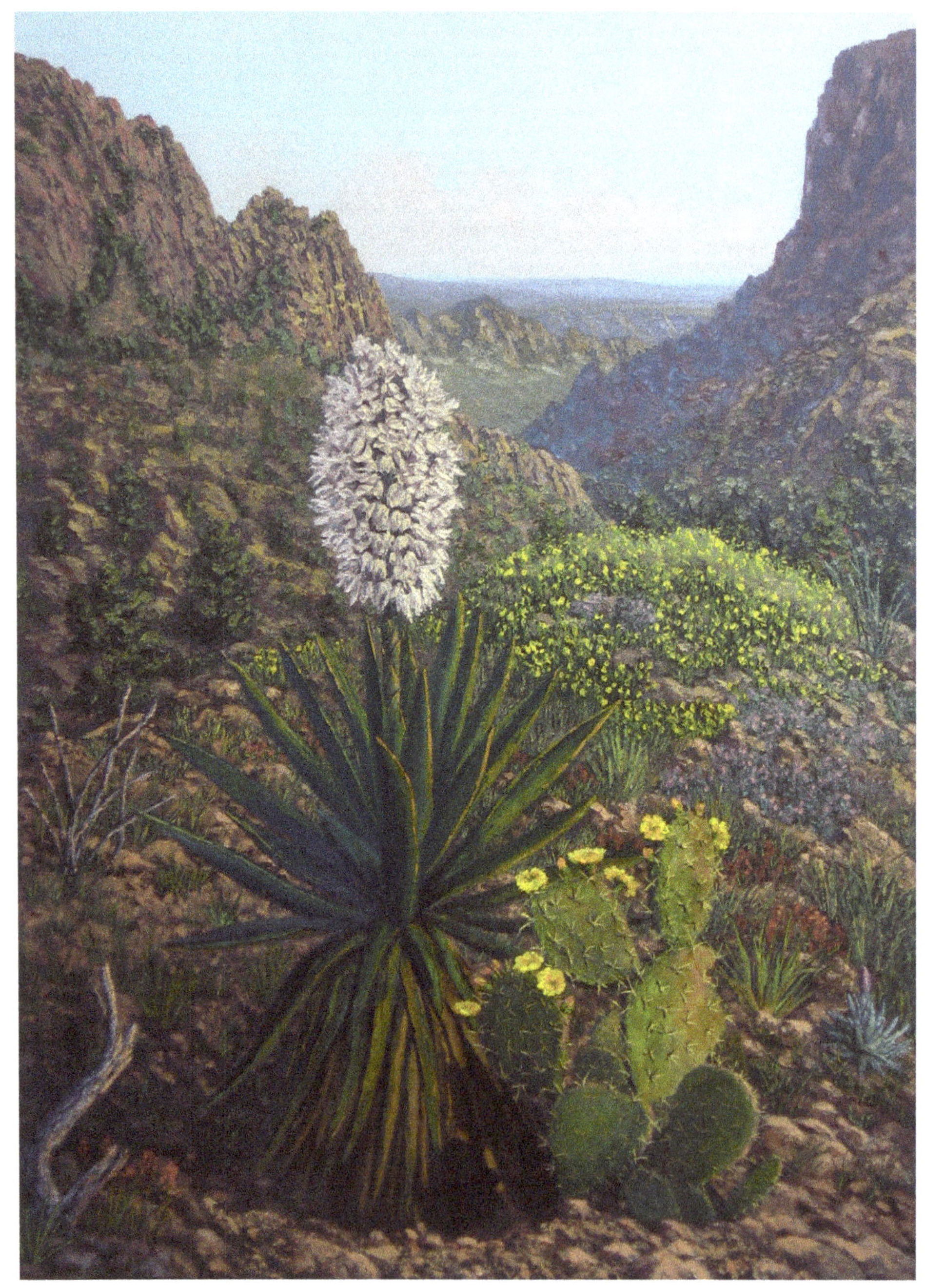

Upland Jewels (18 x 24)

Prickly Pair

Two prickly friends stand
surely too close for comfort
watching the spectacle of
a hoard of mountain daisies
stampeding away over the rocky
hill, then gaze into the blue haze
of the distant valley beyond.
The spiky yucca lifts her white
bonneted head-stalk high to access
the doings far down the shadowed
canyon and spreads her spines
in surprise at something in that farness.
Her cactus companion extrudes
inquisitive golden blooms, nestles
even closer to her lofty friend
and whispers, "Oh, tell me, please tell!"

Other Landscapes and Seascapes

Sea Reflections (6 x 14)

Two Lights to Steer By

misty moon's mandala
disdains dim competition
above fog-cloaked sea

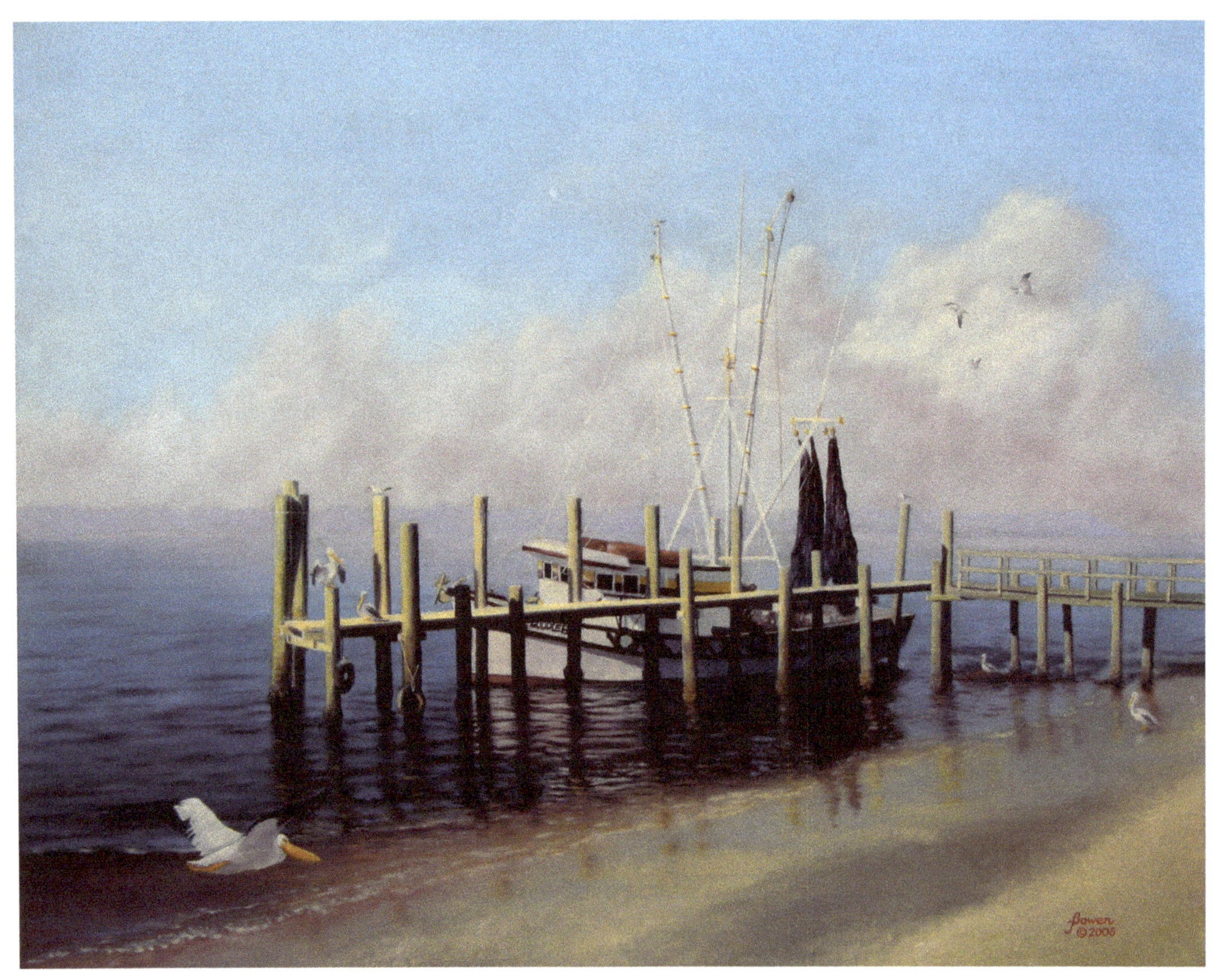

Doodlebug and Friends (11 x 14)

Doodlebug and Friends

The sky is clear and beckoning.
The clouds are bright and billowing.
The breeze is mild and westering.
The water is calm for wandering.

Fresh is my paint.
New are my nets.
Ready my rigging.
Sturdy my lines.

Come perch on these pilings,
you gossipy gulls.
The tide has retreated,
so hike to me, herons.
Glide close, you bucket-beaked,
sky-sliding pelicans.

Let's tell our adventures
while I wait for my crew.
When returned from my shrimping,
I'll share sea's bounty with you.

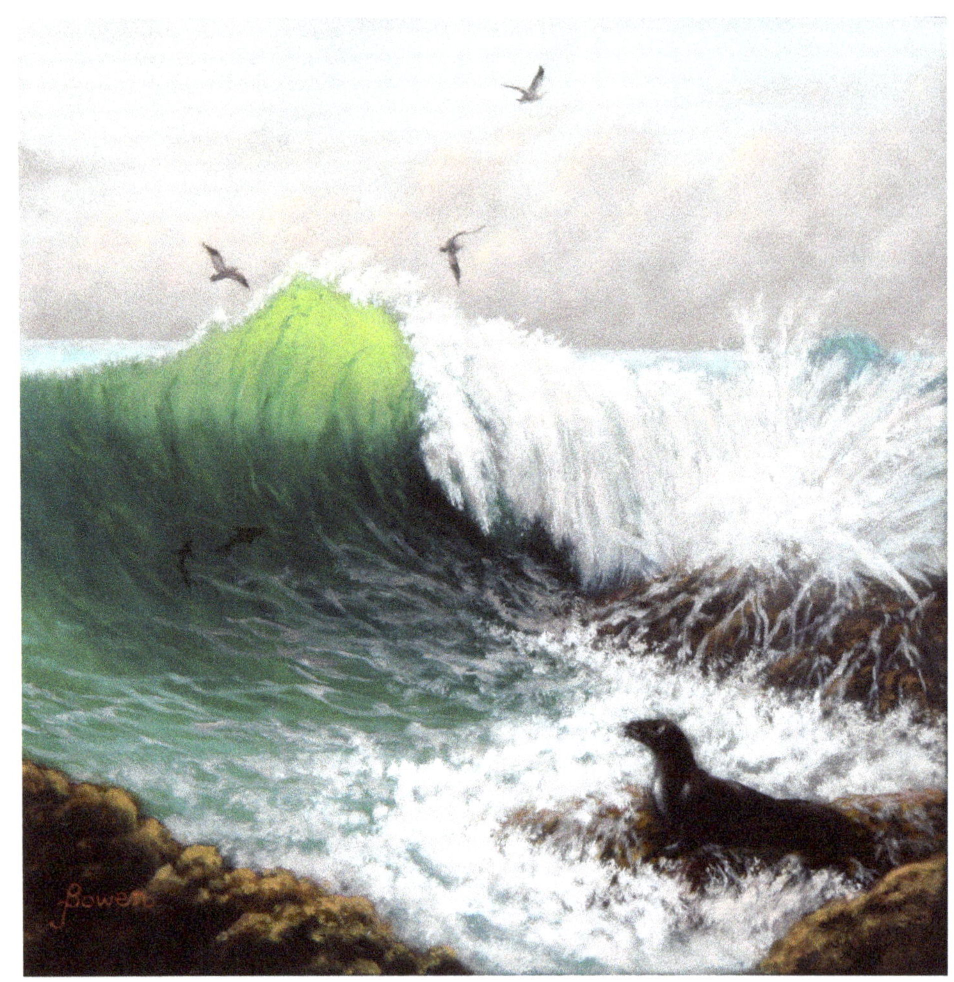

Catch of the Day (5 x 5)

Catch of the Day

Wave rising rolling shattering
gulls careening shrill shrieking
harbor seal tensely considering
fish wave-wandering taunting
black back into green exeunting

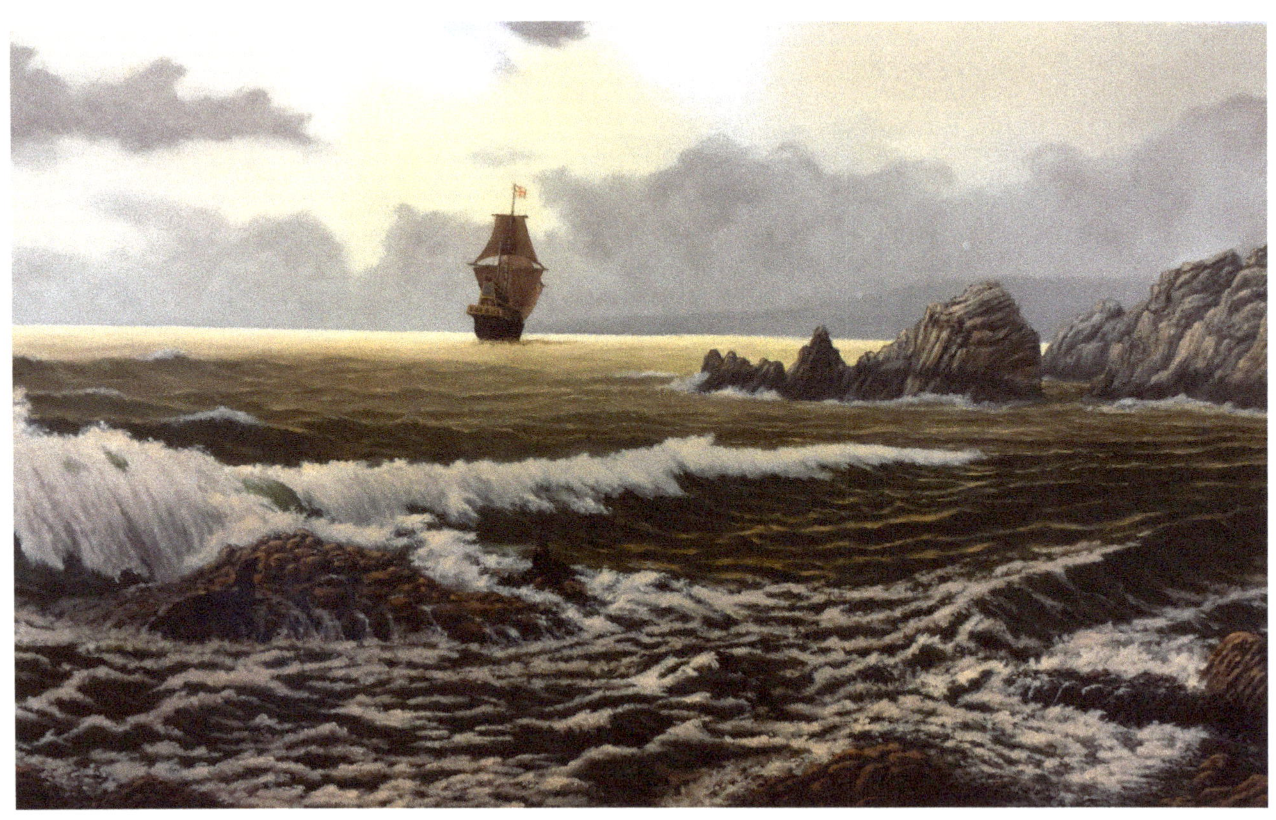

Point Lobos, 1579 (11¾ x 36)

Sir Francis Drake and the Golden Hind

Call him not a pirate but rather privateer.
The Spanish dubbed him *El Draque* in animosity,
for he ranged the Spanish Main many a year,
took ships, bullion, and jewels, from Spain's treasury.

The Spanish sought *El Draque* in fierce animosity,
for, commissioned by Good Queen Bess,
Drake brought millions to her English treasury.
Then, from Panama, he spied the vast Pacific emptiness

and vowed to claim it for Good Queen Bess.
So he sailed from England, the Pelican his flagship,
around Cape Horn into that vast Pacific emptiness,
stealing Spain's *Concepción* treasure for the trip.

Rechristened Pelican, Golden Hind, his sturdy flagship,
three masted galleon, 102 feet by 20, with 22 cannon.
Up west American coast, claimed California at Lobos tip.
Sailed west into the unknown east from what's now Oregon.

His six-ship fleet traversed the immense Pacific to Indonesian
islands, then toward home again around Cape Good Hope,
to complete the first British global circumnavigation.
Drake was knighted, made admiral; wealth and fame his trope.

But Spain was proud and angry, wanted to hang Drake from a rope.
Built their mighty armada to conquer England for revenge.
Drake caught the armada in Cadiz, decimated it in a horrorscope.
King Phillip vowed to rebuild, rearm, and make Great Britain cringe.

The armada's mob made the Chanel throb for Spain to avenge.
But storms and Britain's faster ships brought the armada's demise.
Drake captured an admiral and loot causing Phillip's beard to singe.
Queen Liz consulted her spies, sent Drake to give Spain more surprise.

Drake laid siege to Coruna to inflict armada's remnant's demise.
He harassed Spain still in the Caribbean, her treasure to sever.
Drake died of dysentery off Panama, so close to his Pacific sunrise.
Buried at sea in his armor in a lead-lined coffin, discovered never.

Drake's Golden Hind's a museum ship now, moored in Thames river.
Call him not a pirate, he was the Queen's gallant privateer.
His exploits now legend, he made Britain great and Spain to shiver,
for he ranged the Spanish Main indomitable for many a year.

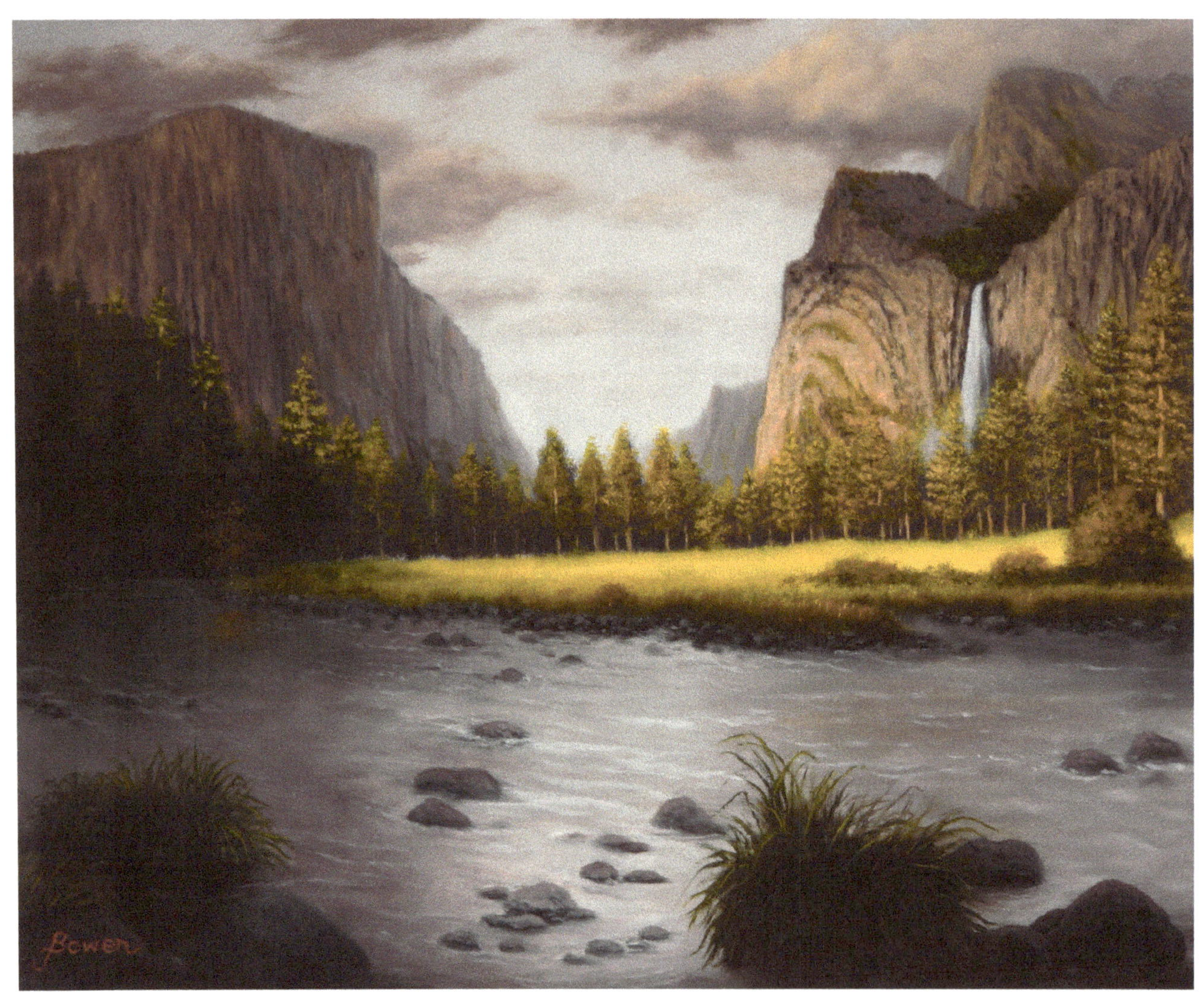

Pride of Yosemite (8 x 10)

Yosemite Sonnet

Ten million years ago these Sierra peaks
were thrust two miles into troposphere
and canted toward the rising sun that seeks
Half Dome and El Capitan when shining here.
Streams cut granite canyons, deep and narrow.
Steep cascades carved hanging vales that capture
snowfall pressed to glaciers in gorge's shadow,
and summer melt forms waterfalls to enrapture
all human eyes that gaze this grand display
from piney woods or Sequoias' titan timber.
Pohono, Spirit of Puffing Wind's misty spray.
Yohhe'meti, means "killer," so *Paiute* remember.
Such awe the view imposes in sublimity,
ironic it was consecrated Yosemite.

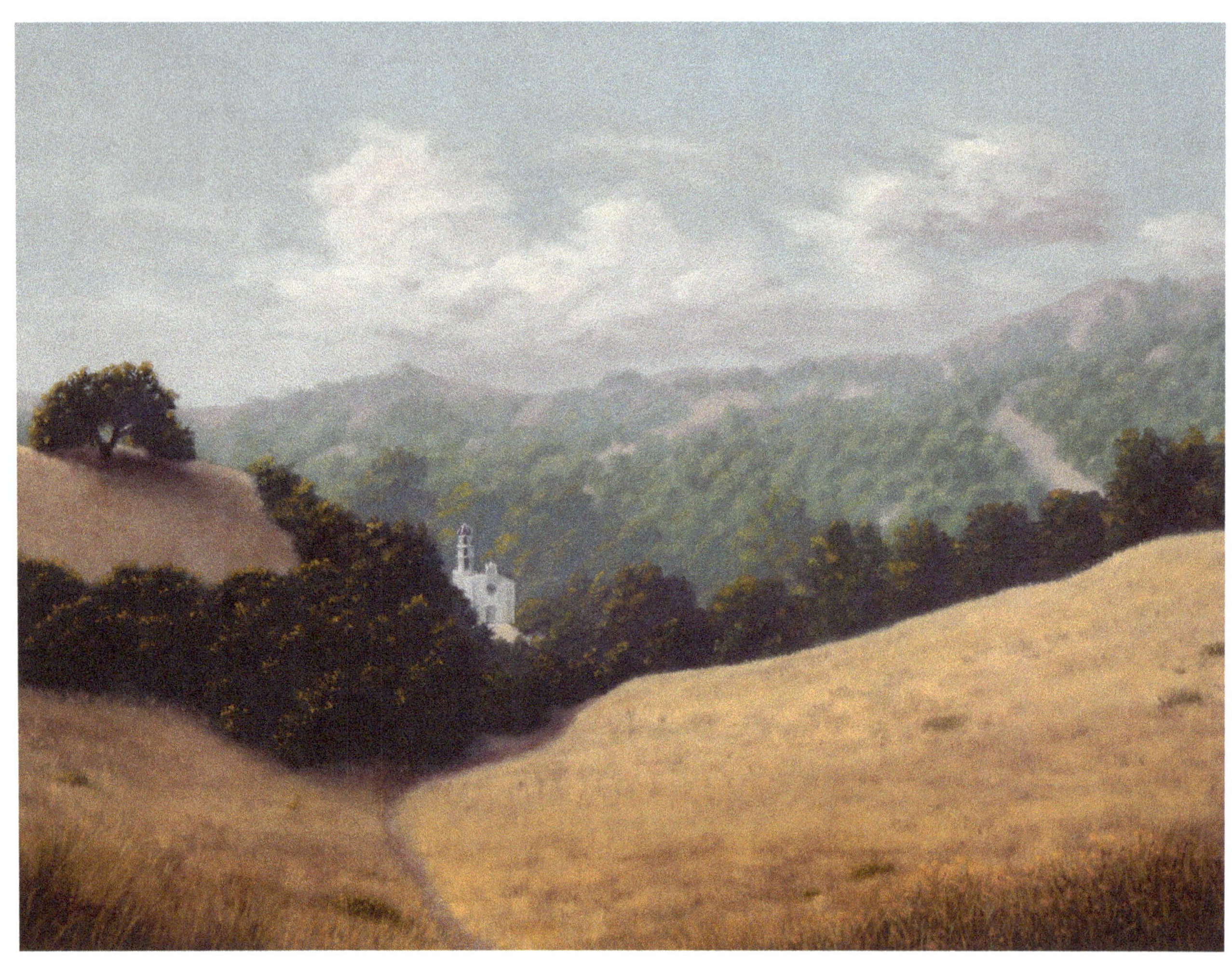

Moraga Morning (10 x 13)

Moraga

A lone tree atop a barren hill,
a tall columned church like
a castle, besieged by dense
green forest, like Birnam Wood
come to Dunsinane.
But this is California, not
the Scottish highlands.
The bright torrid foreground
is empty of all animal life
that should be teeming there.
The woods seem to menace
the church, threatening to
swallow it up, as if it were
the last human structure on
an Earth being reclaimed by
nature during the Sixth Extinction,
the end of our brief Anthropocene,
the relentless sun too much
for a careless, too numerous,
too greedy humanity, which used
the Earth unwisely and too well.

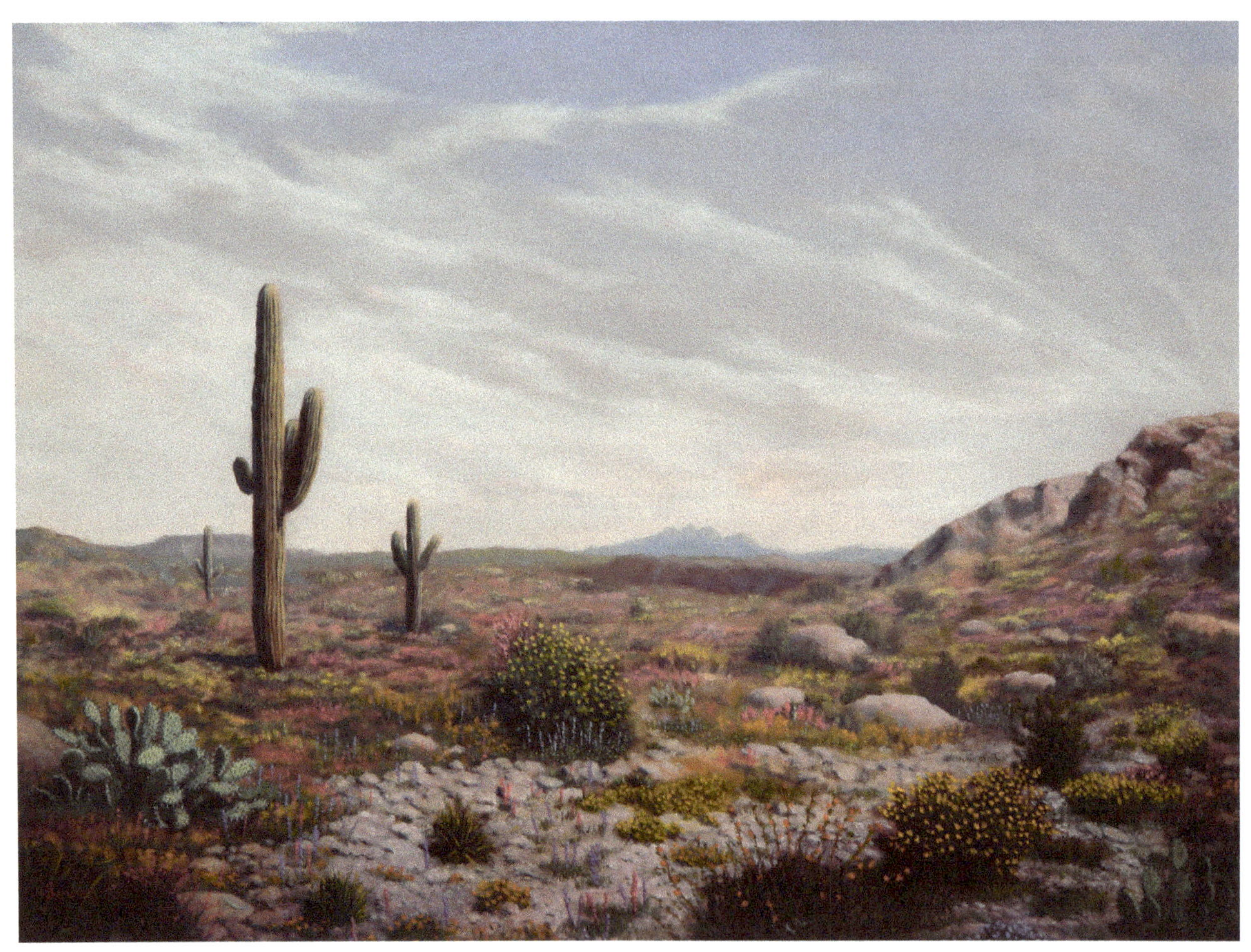

Lizard on a Rock (12x16)

Lizard on a Rock

For some, the desert is a forbidding scene
of sharpness, of hot danger under a harsh,
oppressive sky. Here the Sublime, as awe
and terror, can grip the lone wanderer
with wonder and, for humans, alien anxiety.
You find it too hot, too rugged, too implicit
with possibility for injury. But gaze upon this
scape with an unprejudiced, beauty-creating eye.
Here is multi-hued, many-textured terrain
diverse in size and shape of plant life:
sky-stretching Saguaro swell their barrels,
loft their arms in hallelujah for the rain that
recently dappled the land in motley tints,
Prickly Pear prepare spiny pads to flower,
vari-colored blooms spring from any crevice,
life eagerly explores every exquisite possibility.
And I, being a wise, wily Chuckwalla, find this
the most lovely and practical of places. Indeed,
I must be the luckiest of lizards, soaking up
the morning warmth, enjoying the vivid foliage,
planning my soon exploring among luxuriant flora
of my immense, undisputed domain. And surely
it's too early for the sharp-beaked, rascally
Road Runner yet to be about

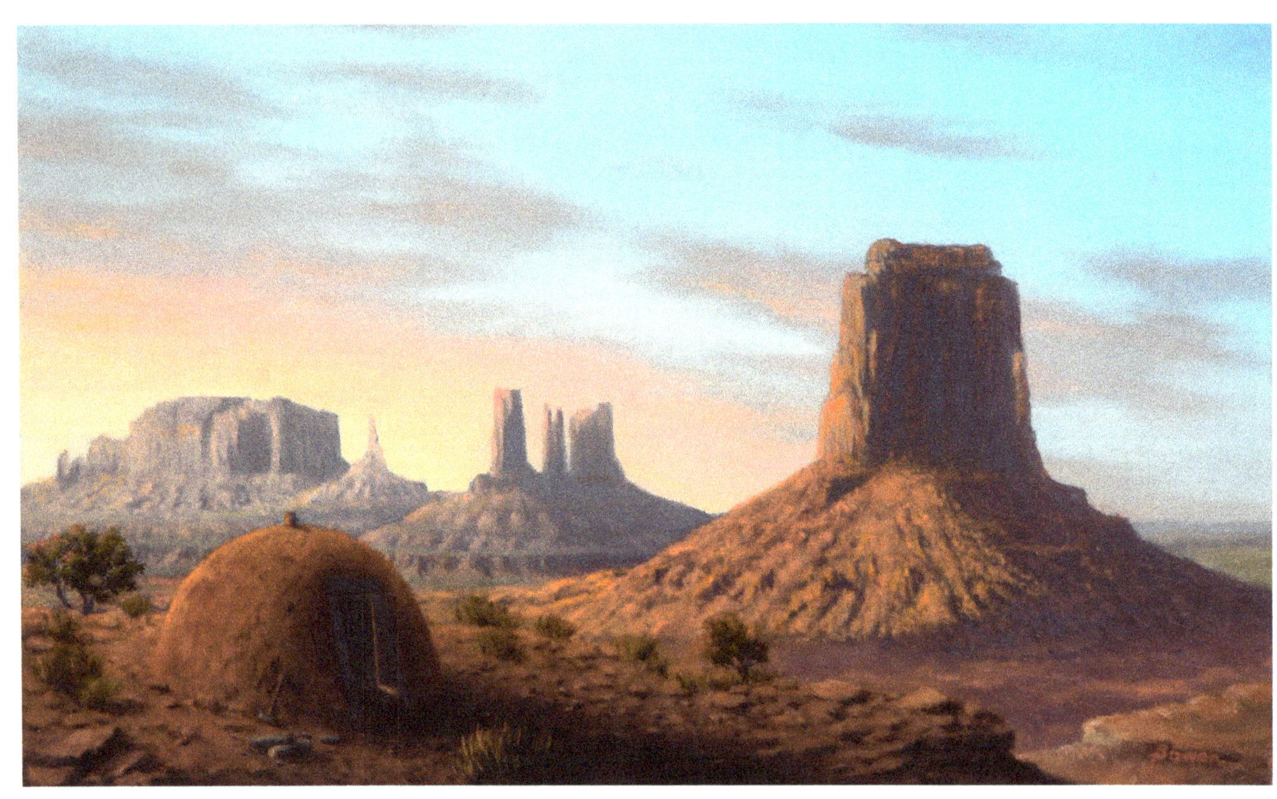

Sacred Place (6 x 10)

Sacred Place

Here, in the high Valley of the Rocks,
these mesas, buttes, and peaks
are stony arms of Earth reaching up
to support the Sky, lair of eagles,
always with awe in this sacred place.
Here, from this blood red earth
will I build my hogan to worship
the Sun, newborn each day, gratefully,
as do the little birds in their bushes,
the butterflies and bees whose wings
sing with sunlight in this sacred place.
And at night I will lie upon warm rock,
listening for the whispers of our ancestor
stars speaking among themselves
of spirit being, of the agony of lostness,
of the blessings of the Beauty Way,
of the ache for a new creation
among these prayerful monoliths,
bones of gods, in this sacred place.

Still Lifes

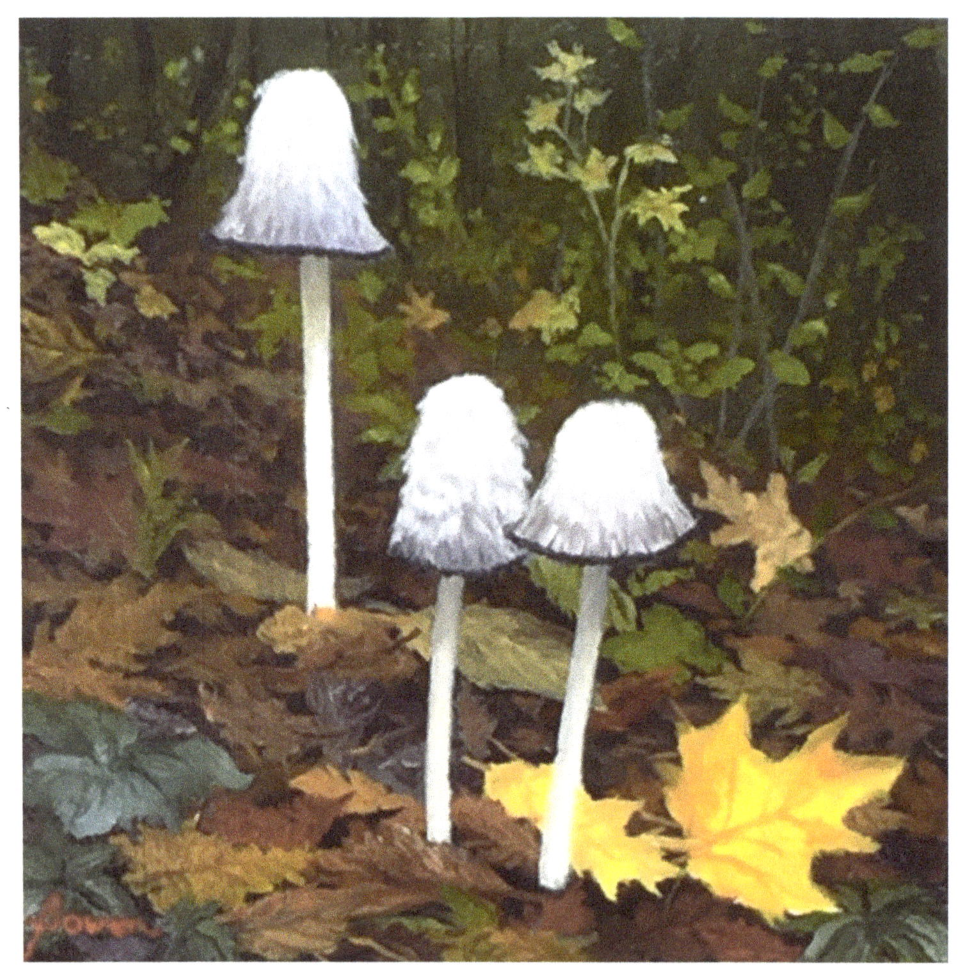

Fruit of the Earth (5 x 5)

A Threnody in Winter

Walking in the woods after visiting the Houston Holocaust Museum

The gaunt moon makes its cold nest in the wind—
A grumpy toad hunkers in a lost summer shoe—
Late daisies limp into winter on toothless unicycles—
Sandhills bow the sky, croaking southlessly—
A sweet gum's yellow star presses to my chest,
then desperately rejoins the leaf storm—
A few new mushrooms struggle bravely up
through decayed manure like naked children—
Skeletal trees, ensnarled by thorn vines,
frighten even the sparrows—
An abandoned burn pile, still smoldering,
exhales smoke flows like writhing shadows—
Pine cone cantatas whisper "*Dies Irae*,"
song of death on the Day of Wrath,
as they scatter thousands of tiny
dead angels' wings—
Now the woods, the wind, the birds are silent—
Soon it will rain,
the rain of forgetting—
Nor will the wind remember—
But the earth—
The earth will always know the truth.

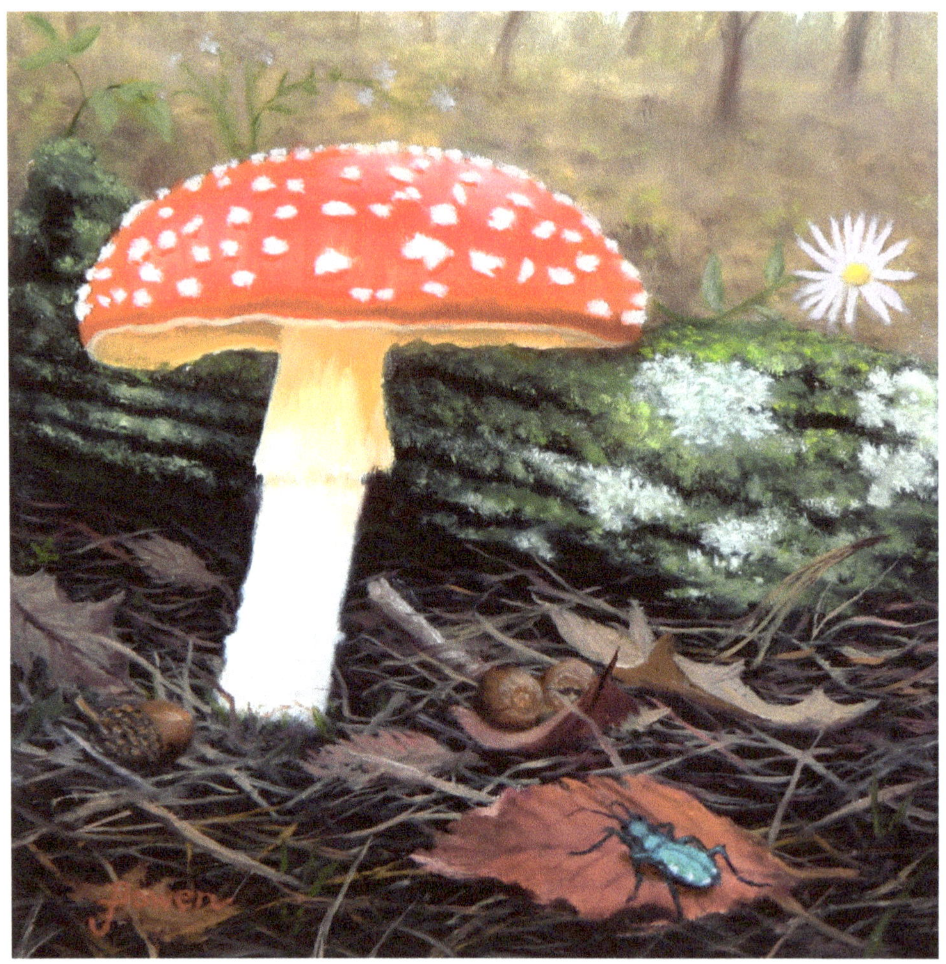

Endless Forms (5 x 5)

Common Magic

The drama of a dandelion
disappearing in the wind,
of flickering fairy lights
on firefly nights,
of winking eyes on wings
of wafting butterflies,
of mud-bubble rainbows, and
beetle knights in shining armor
marching to a mushroom castle.
We world-weary adults too easily
turn such wine into water.
Maybe it takes a five-year-old
to recognize such common magic,
even if she doesn't yet understand
the other name for it is love.

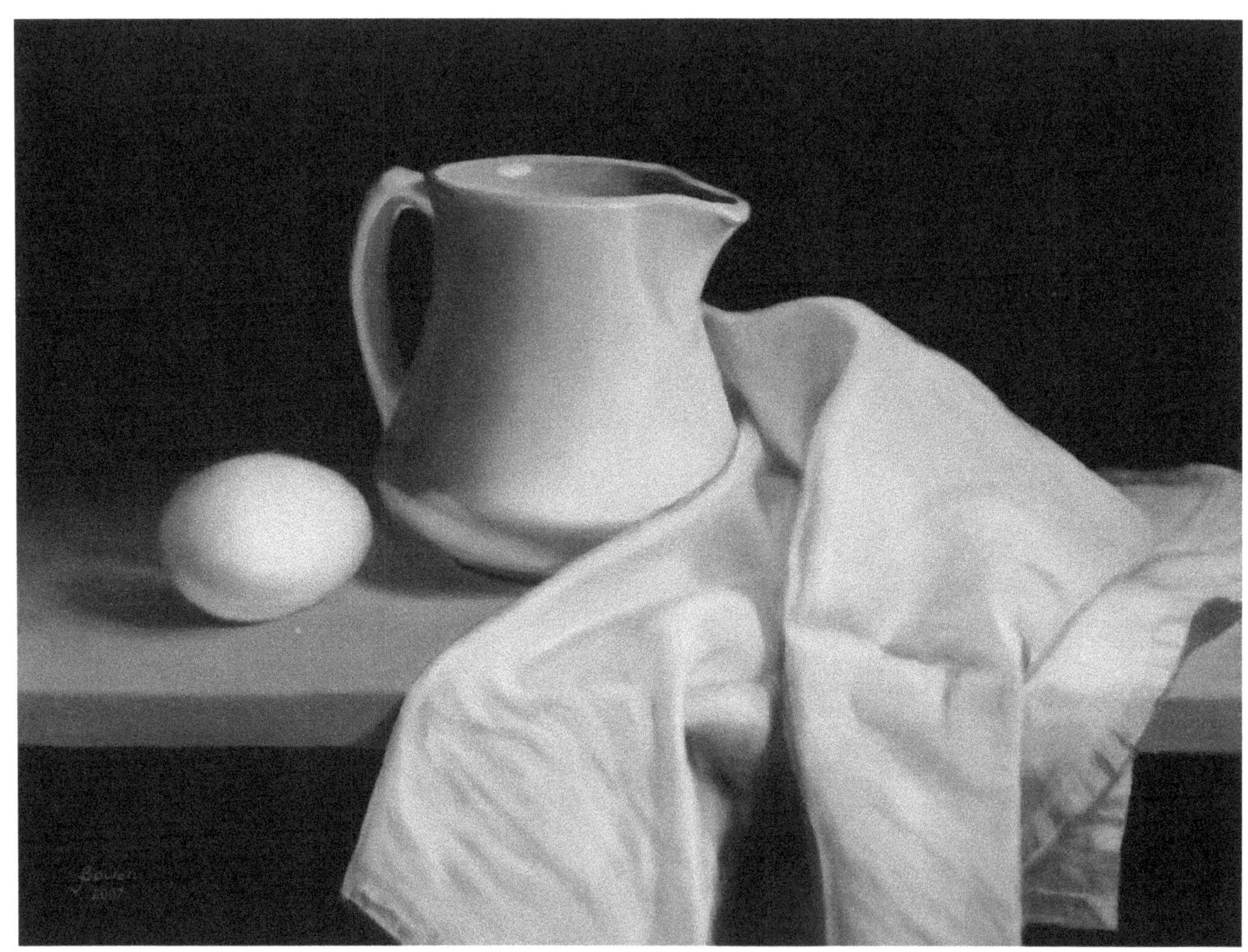

The Why of White (9 x 12)

The Why of White

What is the why of white?
There are so many ways of seeing.
Everything is made of light.

Where there is no day or night,
no floor or wall or ceiling.
What is the why of white?

There is a deepness more than bright,
as if some essence freeing.
Everything is made of light.

What mystery do some things excite?
Might objects' souls elicit this awed feeling?
What is the why of white?

Only truest art can get it right,
this absolute of saying.
Everything is made of light.

Some things require an unseen sight.
They radiate the weight of being.
What *is* the why of white.
Everything is made of light!

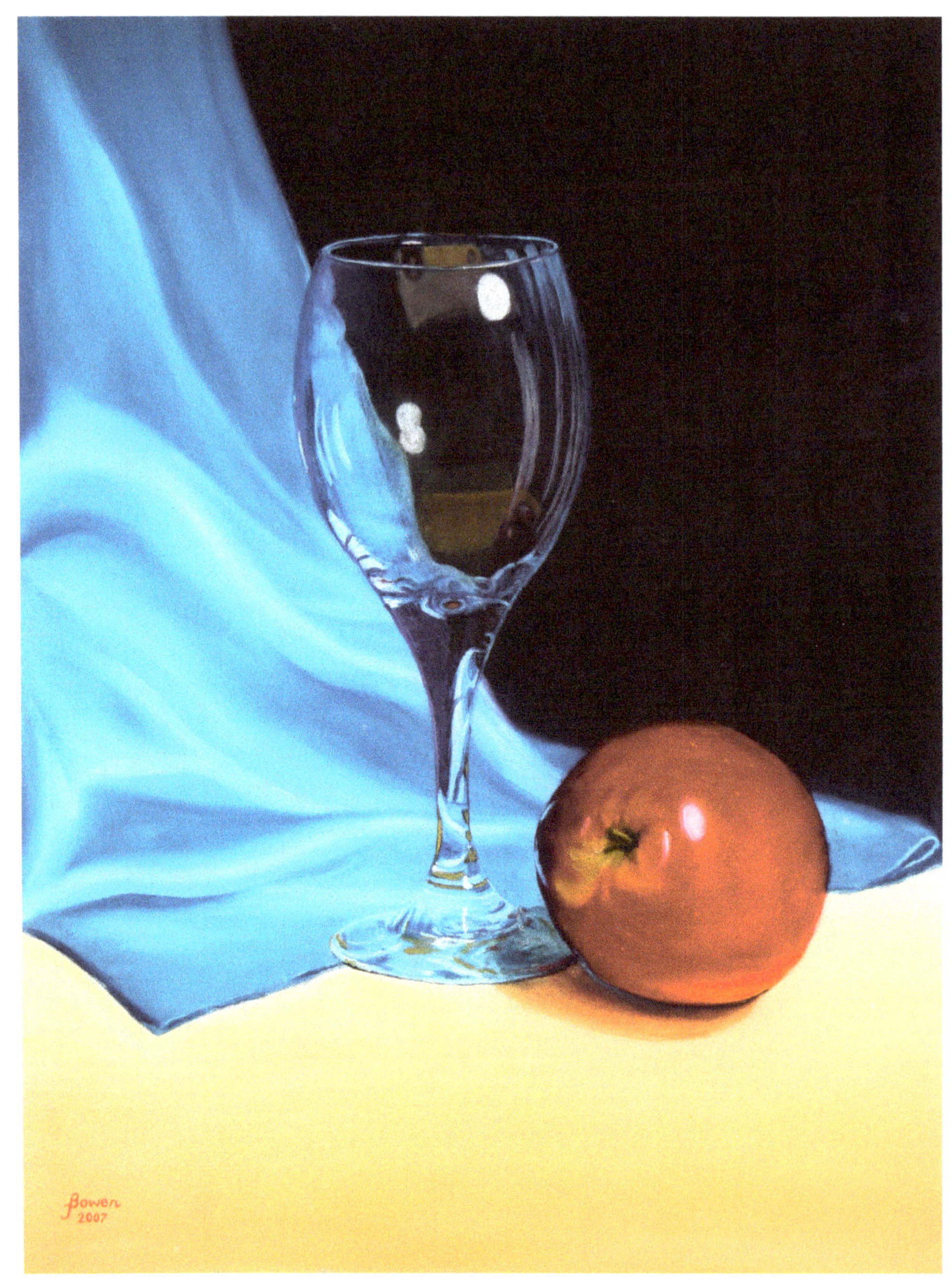

The Odd Couple (10 x 13)

The Odd Couple

She is tall, elegant, sensuously
shapely, exuding a desire
to be held, to be kissed.
She collects the brittle glitter
and excitement surrounding her,
reflecting as bright gossamer
ghosts the images and objects
that seek her.

She is empty of everything but
delight, while he is full of himself:
orotund, opaque, yet radiating
some vast mysterious passion
for becoming he is but barely able
to contain. He has fallen for her,
smitten to the core.

With an empty gravity, she attracts,
refracts, enwraps herself
in an almost royal blue.
He approaches her pedestal,
adoring, worshiping.
And she does not distain him.
She contains him, like a heart,
in the depths of her,
while he is caressed, blessed
by the faint blue blaze
of their osculation.

Never ask how full the glass
nor of the ripeness of the apple.

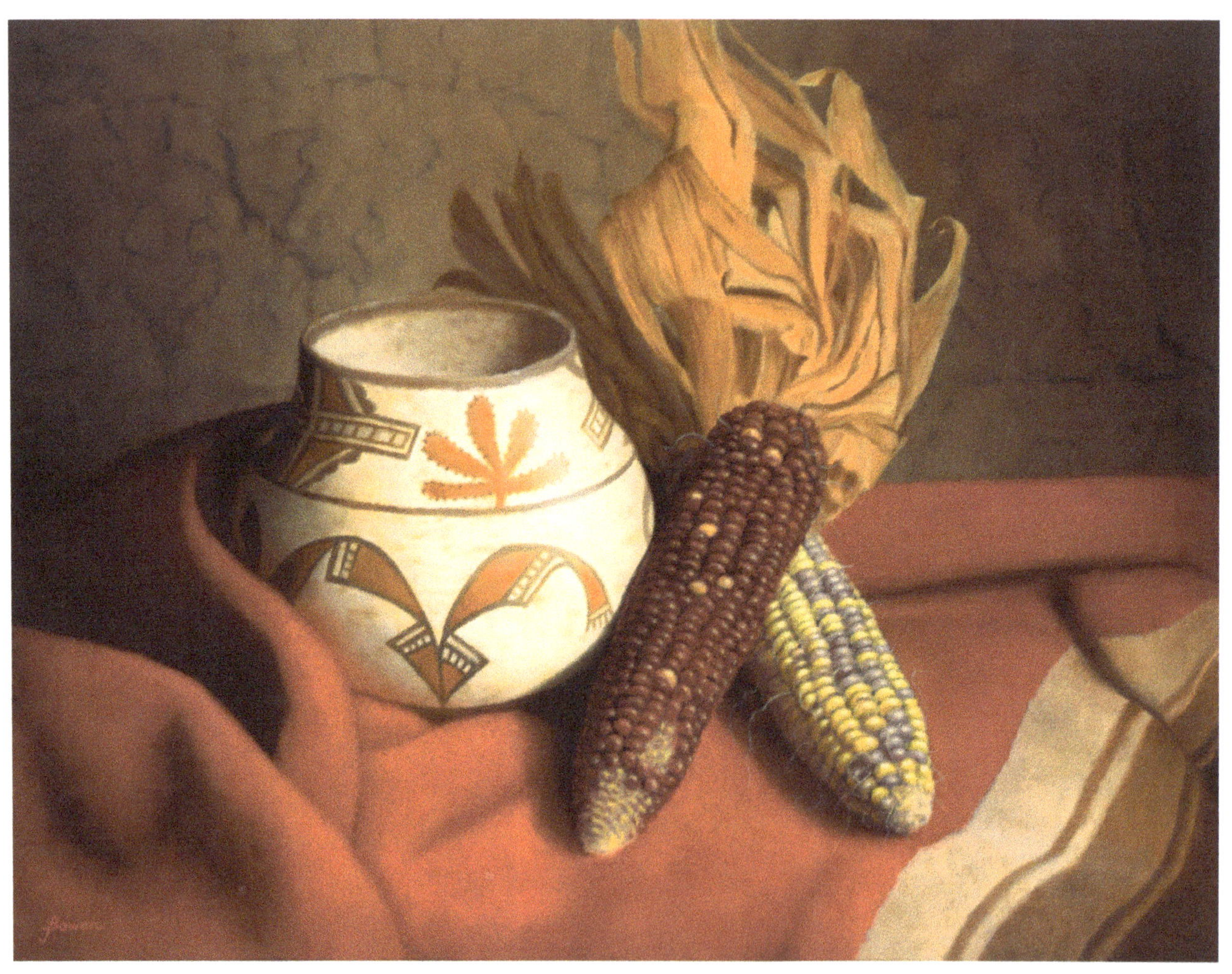

Zuni Memory (12 x 16)

Zuni Pot

A simple clay pot, already ancient when
its tribe first encountered questing Europeans.
Created for some humble mundane purpose, perhaps
to safeguard maize kernels for each next season's planting.

Yet the potter took both
effort and time to decorate, to display
artistic skills requiring a lifetime to acquire,
sacred symbols from millennia of ancestral inherence.

What deep impulse within
us loves design, demands artistry?
Art seized us only forty thousand years ago.
Before, we made implements but did not adorn them.

Suddenly, ornamentation, depictions
of animals, humans, fantasy creatures, gods,
abstract designs upon almost every object we created.
Was our ache for art the mystery that made us fully human?

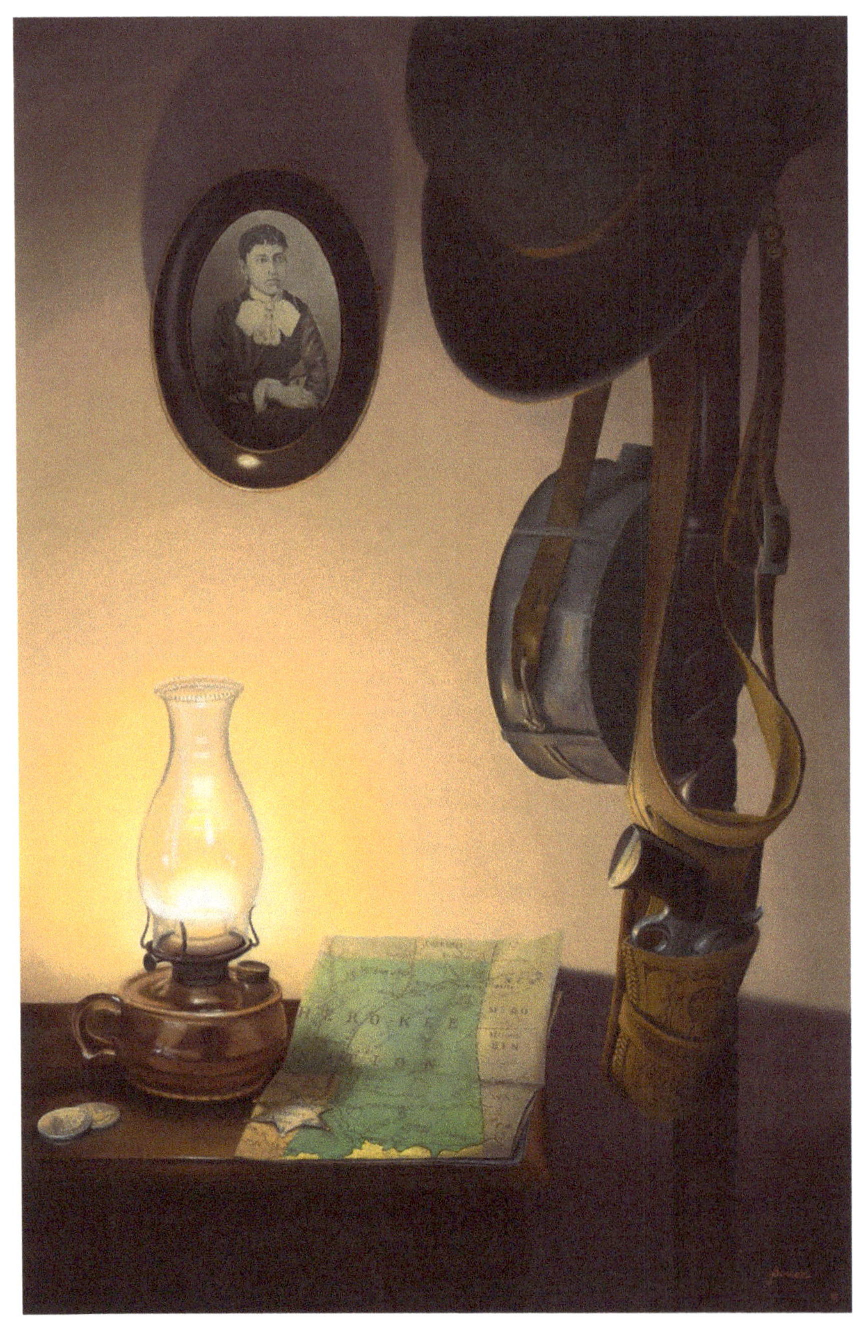

Bass Reeves, Headin' Out (20 x 30)

Granddad Was a Cowboy

When ten I spent a summer with him on his ranch in Denver City, Texas. It was a real adventure for this city boy. He taught me to ride a horse and sling a lasso. I practiced roping fence posts and chairs--most anything that would hold still. We rode together for hours, supposedly checking fence and rounding strays, but I think he mostly enjoyed the peacefulness of the prairie, the bleak beauty of it. It was all exotic to me: cactus, mesquite, sagebrush, tumbleweed, yucca, cedar, inter-sprinkled with wildflowers, thriving in spite of drought and sun-scorch from relentless sky.

One day we drove a few cattle into a corral. He put a cow in a squeezer to be injected with medicinal serum. I wanted to see how cows were branded, but that had been done back in the spring. He asked if I wanted to try bull riding. I would have said yes to anything cowboy. He lassoed a yearling calf, held while I mounted, told me to hang tight, then let it go. I was on the ground four seconds later, having spent two of those in the air. Caught my breath, ready to go again, but he said it might ruin the calf for rodeo.

I had bought my first pair of boots for this visit. They came in handy for more than riding. Walking through a pasture one evening, we got too near a rattlesnake. He heard the rattles whirr and jerked me back just as it struck, recoiling off my boot. It was a small rattler, or might have caught me higher. He always carried a pistol, and quickly dispatched the unlucky varmint. I was more excited than scared. He suggested it wouldn't be necessary to mention the incident to my Mom and Dad.

When my parents picked me up to return home, Granddad presented me with a Winchester 22 rifle. Sporting a heavy octagon barrel, it was some five times older than myself. He said he used it to shoot coyotes from horseback. I loved that gun and hunted rabbits with it myself. A few years later Granddad visited us and borrowed the rifle for a hunting trip. I never saw it or him again.

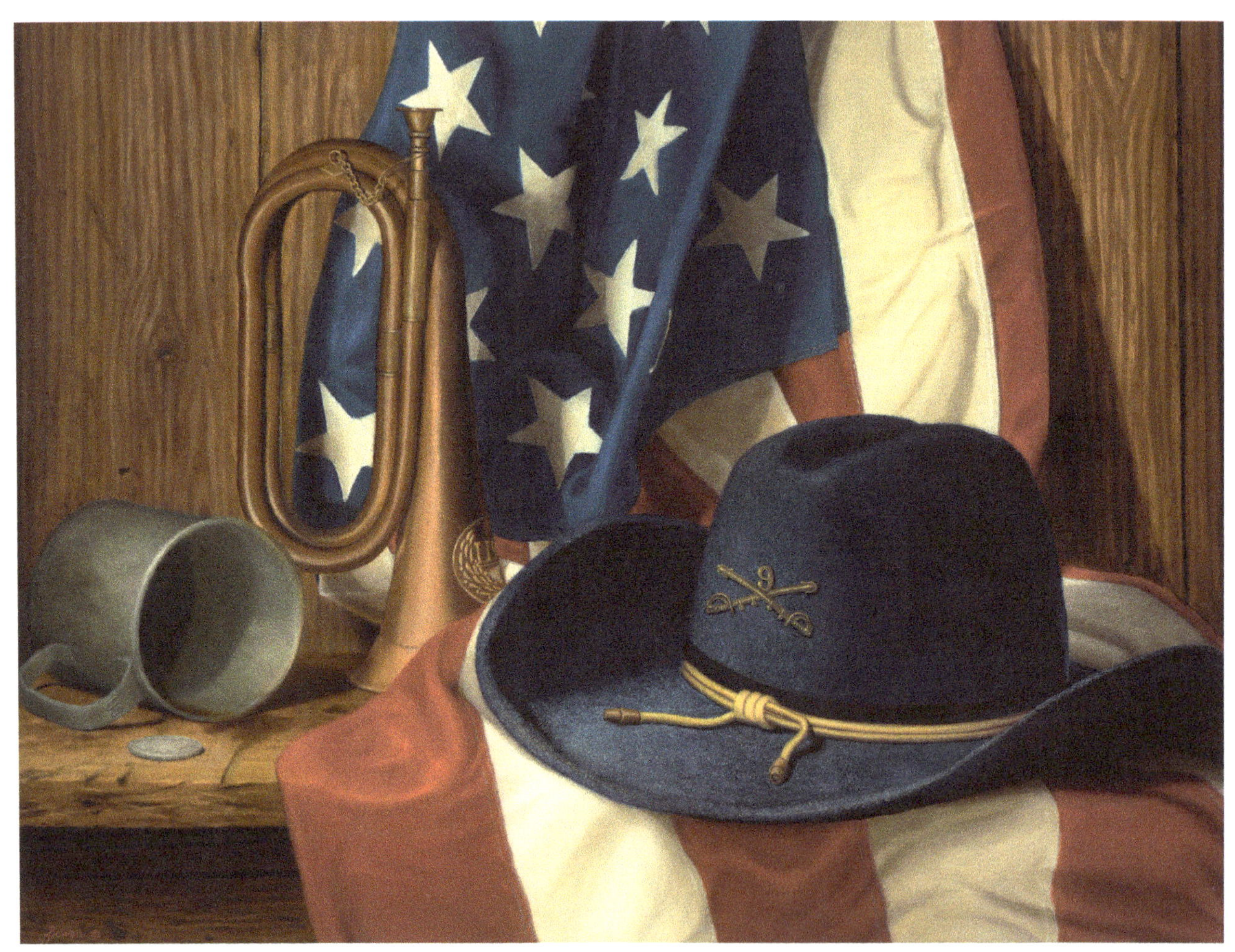

We Can, We Will (18 x 24)

Buffalo Soldiers

After the Civil War, Texas became even more
a cauldron of violence than before.
Outlaws, renegades, and disgruntled rebels
descended on Texas in hoards.
Conflicts between ranchers and farmers boiled.
Mexico seethed at Texas' southern border.
Indians marauded in violent despair
at the overwhelming loss of their culture.
The 9th and 10th U.S. Cavalry were sent into
south Texas to quell the unrest, to make it safe to settle.

These units were known as the Negro Cavalry
by whites but were called the Buffalo Soldiers
by their Indian opponents, because their kinky black hair
reminded Indians of the buffalo mane, and because
they fought with the ferocity of a cornered buffalo.
Stationed various times between 1869 and the late 1870s
at Fort Clark, near Brackettville, Fort Concho, near San Angelo,
Fort Griffin, Fort Richardson, and Fort Davis, they ranged
throughout Texas and the West, fighting Indians, repelling
Mexican revolutionaries, and generally enforcing the peace.
Buffalo soldiers also built forts and roads, strung telegraph lines,
mapped unknown areas, protected the mail, rescued settlers.

They earned nine Medals of Honor during the Indian Wars and went on to fight with Teddy Roosevelt in Cuba, with "Black" Jack Pershing in Mexico, and distinguished themselves in all subsequent Wars as well. But it was as Indian fighters that they gained their name and reputation for fierceness and valor. Texas became settled and prospered in no small measure due to the efforts of the Buffalo Soldiers, who often bore Texans' scorn, both for their race and for their blue uniform. The buffalo above crossed sabers became the symbol patch on their uniforms. Their motto was "We can, we will." They could and they did. The Buffalo Soldiers' exploits now have a proud and honored place in Texas history. Perhaps their ghosts patrol our prairies still.

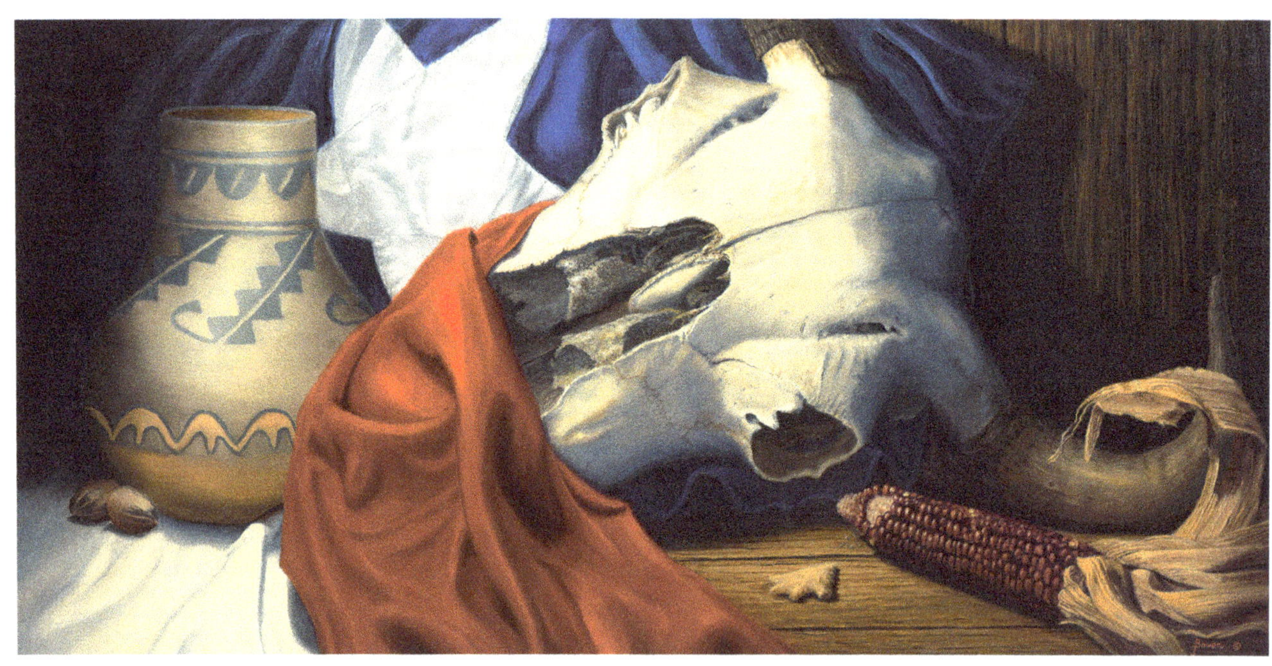

Lone Star Heritage (12 x 24)

Lone Star Heritage

Indians peopled this land when
    mastodons strode the tallgrass prairies.
Conquistadors explored with horse and armor,
    seeking elusive El Dorado.
Missionaries brought the Indians sin,
    sweat, slavery, illness, and despair.
Vaqueros herded longhorns
    among cactus, mesquite, and sagebrush.
Comanche, Apache, Piute, and Sioux
    pursued buffalo on a vast emptiness.
American settlers poured in
    to farm, fence, plow, and plant the rich land.
Pioneer women havened home amid
    heat, cold, wind, drought, dust, and death.
Speculators brought railroads,
    felled forests, mined metals, parceled prairie.
The army arrived to kill the buffalo,
    starve the Indians, pacify the territory.
Ranchers rode in to huge open grasslands
    and fenced it off for cattle.
Merchants, lawyers, bankers came
    to cover it with highways, cities, suburbs.
Wildcatters swarmed like locusts
    to suck black blood from sacred soil.
All these became Texans,
    exploring, exploiting, despoiling, cherishing Texas.
Ghosts of Native Americans
    still haunt the wounded land they loved and lost.

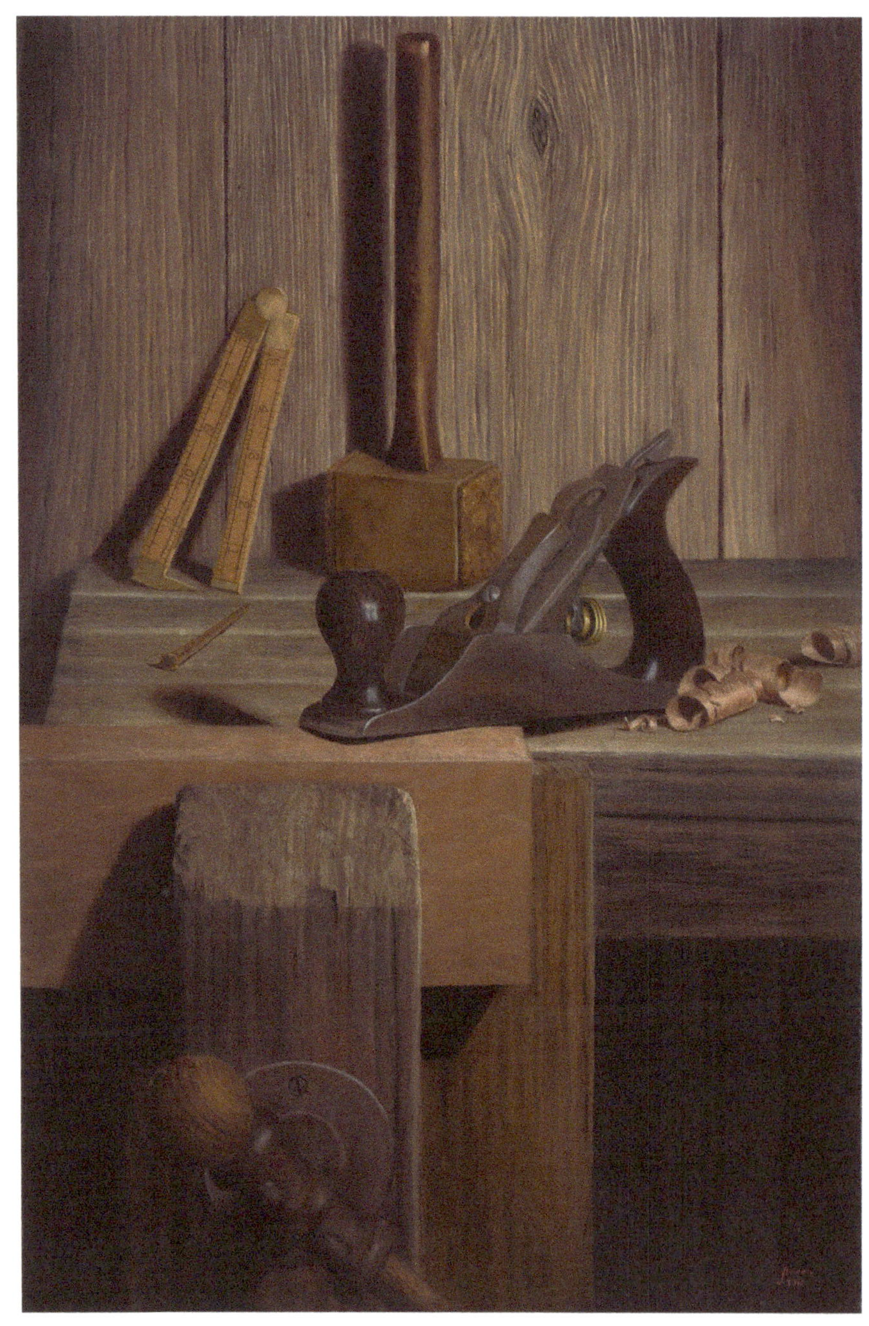

Awaiting His Hands (12 x 18)

Woodworking

Grandad worked with wood,
his movements slow and sure,
never a wasted motion,
shaving and smoothing a block
with such similar gentleness
as he caressed my hair
when I was a hip-high child
watching the shavings curl,
sliding the curls on my fingers,
breathing their pungent aroma,
tightening his vice just so,
helping him take a measure.
He taught me without words
so many deep, loving things.

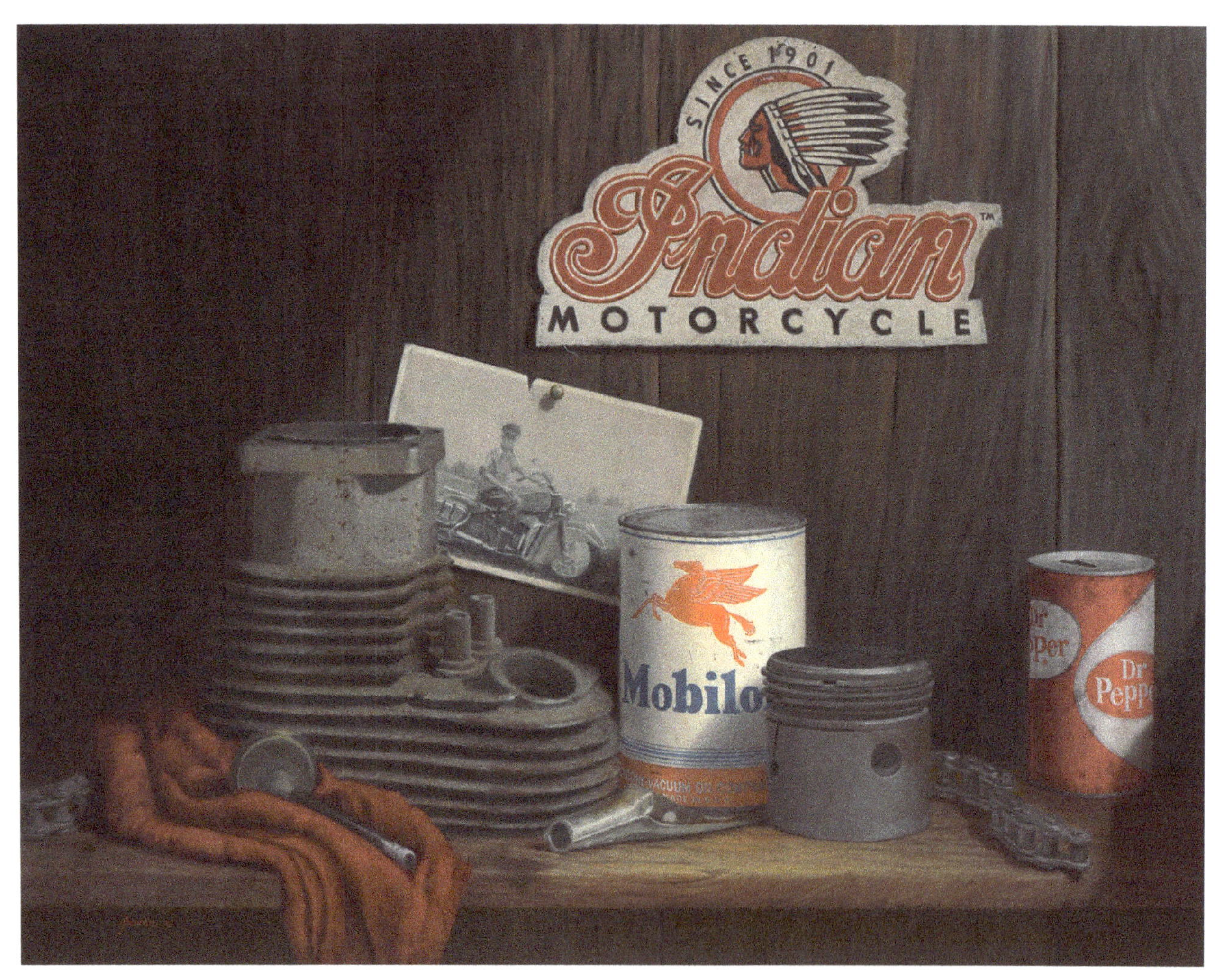

Made in U.S.A. (18 x 24)

Made in U.S.A.

I sputtered into Dalhart,
the wind strong behind me
pushing a dust storm through the berg
and my Indian growling like
a wounded lion between my legs.
Limped into a ramshackle Mobile station
just as the Chief clattered into silence.
"That's a beautiful machine," opined
the ancient geezer wiping off grease.
"I owned an Indian after the War;
best ride ever and made in the USA.
But looks like you got problems."
He rolled down the bay doors against
the storm. We got into the Indian's
metal guts, found the drive chain busted
lucky, just a broken link-pin.
We repaired it while the dust blew through.
Celebrated with cold Dr. Peppers and jawed
on motorcycles, Texas weather, and country
music till the storm wore out. I had made
a friend I'd probably never see again.
But I guess that's what memory is all about,
and, somehow, that one has stuck with me.

Notes from the Poet

Arkansas Landscapes

"*Mysterium Tremendum*"

With this poem I tried to convey the idea of the sublime as fearful mystery as I think Johnny was trying to do with the painting, *Dawn In the Wilderness.* I personified Hawksbill Crag and expressed its awe and terror in leaping out over the deep valley. I thought the bears were a nice touch in the painting to give it some visual perspective.

"Song for Sam's Throne"

When my wife and I drove up to visit Johnny back in the eighties, I had just put a new stereo system in our van, and we really enjoyed its sound on the way up. We stopped on a scenic byway to take in the view. Since we were the only ones there, I positioned the van so I could open its doors and crank up the volume on the stereo to flood the valley below with Vivaldi's *Gloria*. When I saw Johnny's painting of Sam's Throne and heard the story about crazy Sam, I slapped the two together for the poem, omitting the actual playing of the music in deference to the man in the painting.

"Stillness At War Eagle Crossing"

When viewing the painting, I was immediately struck by the curve of the bridge being echoed by the curve of the heron's body. The poem takes off on that idea and offers a meditation on stillness as both the bird and the bridge are caught in a moment of utter calm just before the bird strikes.

"Buffalo River Nocturne"

I love Johnny's way with this night scene (*Moonlit Serenity*) and that of *Steel Creek Sonata*. The natural world is so different at night and is made magical by moonlight. I tried to capture that idea of moon magic in the poem.

"Ancient Sentinel"

I often use personification of inanimate objects in my poems, as I did in this case with the rock and tree. Paradoxically, it often allows me to explore ideas of human emotion more effectively than if I were doing so with humans.

"The Journey"

Poems that simply describe a work of art don't do much for the reader because they can appreciate the art for themselves without the help of a literary description. I usually try to let the painting evoke ideas and emotions that I put into the poem. In this case, there is no description of the painting (*Ozark Memory*) at all. I use it only to help the reader consider journeys both in life and of life.

"On Golden Pond"

This is one of my favorite poems based on one of my favorites among Johnny's paintings—the pervasive golden hue of the painting, the dead trees reflected in the pond, and the ducks descending only to be slaughtered. In the poem, I tried to relate the autumnal beauty, the poignancy of the situation, and the frisson of fear the ducks might feel as they realize they have been tricked.

"Peace at Old Arkansas Bridge"

This painting (*Peaceful Crossing*) is very similar to Johnny's other bridge picture (*War Eagle Crossing*) without the heron. How to make them different? I concentrated on how the function of the bridge changed when it was abandoned to nature and became a refuge for animals, and for us if we seek to create a peaceable kingdom.

"Silent Night in Boxley"

This is a simple poem about a simple painting. The essence of the painting for me is the bright whiteness of the snow. The unseen moon must be causing the snow to glow. Everything in the picture is silently active and sublime.

"Staring up the Stars"

As a former amateur astronomer, I've always been awed and amazed by the night sky, especially in the mountains where Johnny lives. The hypnotic effect of viewing the stars always causes my mind to wander, just as I'm sure it did the Native Americans who believed their ancestors became stars, and that's how this poem originated.

"Steel Creek Sonata"

It amazes me that Johnny's night paintings can combine tranquil beauty with blazing light. I tried to convey that contradiction in the poem. Perhaps we tend to find the human face in almost any random pattern, but the face in the cliff looking at the moon was just too good to omit from the poem.

"Abandoned Hay Bales"

I can't resist personification in a painting like this. It immediately brought to mind a stage play with the hay bales as actors. I combined that idea with the feeling that these bales have somehow been forgotten and are sad at their abandonment.

"View of Boxley Valley"

I love the immense vista of this painting. But what got my poetic imagination flowing was the foreground with the sunbeam illumining the grassy area before the vista. Looking closely you can see the variety of flowers and vegetation that Johnny depicted but which gets overlooked for the more dramatic aspect of the painting. I researched flowers of that area and used particularly striking names in the poem. Then I realized the sunbeam would move from that spot and the rest of the poem evolved from that idea.

Texas Landscapes

"Speak, Water"

What tales a stream could tell if it could talk, and perhaps it can if we knew how to listen. So many of Johnny's paintings have wonderful lone trees in them. This one seems to be leaning over to listen to the stream. That's what got the poem started for me.

"Gonna Be a Hot One"

These old sheds with corrugated iron roofs are ubiquitous in rural Texas. They have a dilapidated dignity that makes them picturesque and are perfect subjects for both paintings and poetry. You know there's something interesting inside. As a kid I loved to investigate them. The red wasps also loved them. Notice that the poem is one long sentence except for the last line.

"Wildflower Witness"

Johnny's painting *Spring Tonic* is one of the first he ever showed me and is still one of my favorites. It immediately inspired this poem. Here again is one of Johnny's fabulous lone trees. I've had lots of people claim they've seen this same chimney in various places in Texas, so there must have been a lot of pioneer cabins that left only the hearth standing. Can't you just smell the coming rain from that storm cloud?

"Chisos Splendor"

Johnny makes desert scenes almost as inviting as his lush mountain meadows. I was intrigued by the yucca plants depicted in the painting. In researching them for the poem, I found they were widely used by Indians of the southwest for food, clothing materials, etc. But it was their mode of reproduction that really caught my attention as a student of natural history. So a major element of the poem is the fact that yucca require moths to lay eggs in the seeds to help them germinate.

"Mustangs"

Instead of writing a poem about the particular ranch and horses Johnny depicted in *Texas Tranquility*, I decided to write about the history of the horse in Texas. At the time, I was writing a book of poetry that leaned heavily on Texas history, so Johnny's painting created that opportunity.

"Pastoral Pastiche"

I obviously tried something a bit different with this poem. Instead of telling a story, I carefully examined the various features of the painting *Johnny's Spot* and listed them in pairs using rhyme and alliteration as the primary poetic elements.

"Utopia, Texas"

In this poem, I decided to riff on the name of the area depicted as well as the elements of the landscape itself. That led to the meaning of utopia and to the Thomas Moore novel. That, in turn, reminded me that this sort of landscape is what early humans found optimal and it has influenced our sense of beauty and desirability since prehistoric times.

"Llano Estacado"

This is another poem I wrote for my book, *Lone Star Heart: Poems of a Life in Texas*. I thought Johnny's painting *Prickly Pears* was appropriate to pair with the poem because the painting is a close up showing just earth, cactus, and sky, which are the primary elements of the Llano Estacado. The painting itself is different from most of Johnny's work and effectively expresses the heat and harshness of the Llano Estacado.

"Prickly Pair"

I wanted to inject some humor into a poem for a change of pace, and the painting *Upland Jewels* lent itself to that desire. This painting is similar to *Chisos Splendor*, so I wanted to make the poem different from the rather serious one for the previous painting. The closeness of the two plants generated the idea that they might be friends gossiping with each other.

– Other Landscapes and Seascapes –

"Two Lights to Steer By"

This is a standard haiku with three lines and a 5,7,5-syllable structure. The idea of competition between the moon and the lighthouse came quickly. The picture itself is deceptively simple. I wanted to match that simplicity with an equally modest poem.

"Doodlebug and Friends"

I decided to make the shrimp boat the main character in this poem and let him do all the talking. He's a jolly, enthusiastic chap who cheers all those around him.

"Catch of the Day"

I love the look of the wave in this painting. I wanted to convey the action, excitement, and tension of this single moment as the wave is crashing and about to crash. Thus it had to be a short poem, every line expressing a different action in that moment.

"Sir Francis Drake and the Golden Hind"

The poem is a pantoum, a form in which the second and fourth lines of each stanza are repeated or echoed by the first and third lines of the next stanza. The first and third lines of the first stanza are repeated as the second and fourth lines of the last stanza to bring the poem full circle. I was somewhat surprised when I first saw the painting *Point Lobos, 1579* because it is rather different from most of Johnny's work. But it's a beautiful painting and is relevant for me because I visited London in 2014 and saw the Golden Hind replica docked on the Thames.

"Yosemite Sonnet"

I wanted to do more than just respond to the beauty of Johnny's painting, *Pride of Yosemite*. So I researched the history of the park and decided to use the Indian names for the waterfall and the park itself. The poem is a Shakespearian sonnet with the standard fourteen lines and an alternating line rhyme structure with the last two lines, the envoy, rhyming and providing a summing up.

"Moraga"

This beautiful painting put me in mind of Macbeth, with the trees seeming to advance on the church. I also had the idea that the expanse of empty, sunny foreground could be a result of global warming.

"Lizard on a Rock"

This is another of Johnny's desert paintings that makes you want to be there. It's also humorous because the lizard is very hard to find. I tried to pick up on that humor by having the landscape described from the lizard's point of view.

"Sacred Place"

I think Johnny really caught the magnificence of Monument Valley. I tried to relate the poem from the point of view of the Navaho shaman inhabiting the hogan.

Still Lifes

"A Threnody in Winter"

This is a poem I wrote many years ago when I lived near Houston. It was not written to go with the painting *Fruit of the Earth*, but I think the two are a good fit since the poem refers to mushrooms like naked children and autumn leaves such as those in the painting. I think the painting lends itself well to the somber mood of the poem.

"Common Magic"

This is another poem I wrote without having the painting *Endless Forms* in mind, but it fits well with the mushroom and beetle images.

"The Why of White"

This is an older poem that I wrote specifically for this painting; Johnny titled the painting after the poem. I felt some spiritual response when I first saw this painting and tried to convey it in the poem. The poem is a villanelle, which requires two repeated lines in alternating stanzas. This form creates an emphasis that for me is mystical, mysterious, and awe-inducing.

"The Odd Couple"

I was taken by the complex simplicity of this painting and wanted to make sure people viewing it would look closer and see the sly details. The apple could have been painted by Degas. I wanted the reader, who hadn't yet seen the painting, to be unsure what or who was being described until the last two lines.

"Zuni Pot"

This poem is a little meditation on art and its function for humanity. I structured it in a stair-step pattern just to make it more visually interesting.

"Grandad Was a Cowboy"

This poem is from my *Lone Star Heart* book. I hope it fits with the frontier, cowboy spirit of the painting *Bass Reeves, Headin' Out* even though it wasn't written in response to the painting. I think my grandad and Bass Reeves would have gotten along just fine. The poem is a prose poem, where each line is taken to the right margin rather than enjambed or broken off before the margin.

"Buffalo Soldiers"

I wrote this poem in response to Johnny's painting *We Can, We Will*, and I did considerable research on the Buffalo Soldiers in the process. I wasn't aware of their provenance or accomplishments and was duly impressed. They are an important part of Texas history.

"Lone Star Heritage"

This poem tries to encapsulate the historical heritage of Texas by mentioning each group of people who figured in Texas history and their particular contribution to it.

"Woodworking"

My father was an avid and consummate hobbyist woodworker. He built some furniture, but it was the small wooden puzzles and toys he made for his children and grandchildren that I most remember. I started to make the poem about him but decided it should be more generic so almost anyone can relate to it. This is a non-rhyming sonnet in iambic trimeter.

"Made in U.S.A."

Johnny told me the story behind this painting, so I wanted to incorporate it in the poem to the extent possible. But I also wanted the poem to be one that would have wide appeal. So I told a little story that included the name of Johnny's teacher, the Indian motorcycle, and some of the objects in the painting.

Notes from the Artist

Arkansas Landscapes

Dawn in the Wilderness

Whitaker Point, also known as Hawksbill Crag, is probably the most iconic, most photographed geologic feature in Arkansas. It is located in the wilderness area of the headwaters of the Buffalo National River. My goal in this painting was to contrast the sunlit hills of the early morning, with the still-in-shadows outcrop and surrounding trees. A she-bear and her two cubs must soon vacate the overlook, as two-legged visitors will soon start to intrude on their privacy.

Summer Sunset at Sam's Throne

This beautiful view is located near Mount Judea in Newton County. It is in the Buffalo National River watershed and is a popular hiking and rock climbing destination. It was on this conical mountain that, in the 1820s, a settler named Sam Davis climbed and preached to no one in particular after his sister was allegedly kidnapped by local Indians. My wife, Peggy, can be seen looking out at the vista while a red-shouldered hawk watches for rodents to feed her fledglings.

War Eagle Crossing

Named for an Indian chieftain, War Eagle Creek is a major tributary of the White River in northwest Arkansas. In the 1930s the old bridge was constructed by the Civilian Conservation Corps. Now abandoned, the bridge and the creek are a sanctuary for wildlife and anglers. A great blue heron finds a tasty meal in a quiet pool.

Moonlit Serenity

My first night-scene painting. It is a composite of my recollections of the Buffalo River. Two elk hide in the shadows.

Ancient Sentinel

This gnarly pine is hundreds of years old. It is on the bluff facing Sam's Throne and is included in my painting *Summer Sunset at Sam's Throne*. Between my first visit to Sam's Throne and a later visit to photograph the pine tree, someone broke off one of the lower limbs. In my painting, I restored the limb. The valley below drains into Big Creek, a tributary of the Buffalo River. A few years ago, the state of Arkansas approved a permit for a huge hog farm operation along Big Creek. After much public outcry and after the hog farm had been in operation for several years, the permit was finally revoked. The Buffalo River and its tributaries are among the most pristine watersheds in Arkansas.

Ozark Memory

My third painting, which I kept and now hangs in our bedroom. My wife, Peggy, thinks of it as "the road to home." If one drives to the Steel Creek Campground on the Buffalo River, there is a steep, paved road that goes down into the valley. This painting represents what it might have looked like when European settlers first came to the valley. My composition was influenced by a painting by Asher Durand.

Gillett Farms Mallards

My first commission painting, made for a banker who duck hunts near Gillett, Arkansas. Visiting the site, I wore waders to get the reference photos for the painting. I also had to learn a lot about ducks. For example, as ducks start to land, they raise special feathers on the leading edges of their wings, helping them to stall and land gently in the water.

Peaceful Crossing

Another painting of the old bridge over War Eagle Creek. A very limited palette was used.

Silent Night in Boxley

I transformed my photo of the historic Boxley Baptist Church into a winter scene. The constellation Cygnus, also known as the Northern Cross, is in the upper right.

Eternal Lights

Boxley Baptist Church and cemetery lie within the beautiful Boxley Valley in the upper reaches of the Buffalo River. The valley and farmsteads are now part of the Buffalo National River and are protected from future development.

Steel Creek Sonata

This night scene is at the Steel Creek campground on the Buffalo River, a great place to camp, fish, and swim in the cool, clear water.

Hay Bales along the West Fork

The White River headwaters are in the rugged hills of Newton County, Arkansas. As it winds its way westward, it is joined by the Middle Fork east of Fayetteville and then joined by the West Fork a short distance downstream. The town of West Fork sits astride the same-named river and has a beautiful city park, appropriately named Riverside Park. Adjoining the park is a hayfield that I walked past one late summer morning. I took photos of the hay bales and made this painting in a very limited palette. It was accepted into the 2009 Arts Center of the Ozarks regional show and sold there.

View of Boxley Valley

This view, looking west, is from a clearing about 500 feet above the valley. The Boxley Baptist Church, one of my favorite painting subjects, lies below, surrounded by hay fields and the Buffalo River. This clearing has an old, rusting logging truck near the big tree in the foreground, but I left it out of the painting. I have since regretted that decision.

Texas Landscapes

The Old Fishing Hole

This painting could be in Texas Hill Country; the area there is definitely not like the muddy creeks I used to fish in east Texas. My dad, who grew up in Hunt County, used to "noodle" catfish by getting in the muddy water and sticking his arm into hollow logs until he felt a catfish. Then he would grab the catfish and pull it out of the water.

Gonna Be a Hot One

This is a painting of my old barn, transplanted to a Texas landscape.

Spring Tonic (15 x 18)

The chimney in this painting is located at Devils Den State Park in northwest Arkansas. It was built by the Civilian Conservation Corps in the 1930s and was the chimney for the Rec Hall that served the workers while they built the trails, dams, and cabins in the park. I placed the chimney in Texas Hill Country, and the scene depicts the grateful wildflowers after a spring shower. A deer is also enjoying the refreshed landscape.

Chisos Splendor

My first job out of college landed me in El Paso, and I spent a lot of time exploring the desert around there and further down the Rio Grande in Big Bend. The Chisos Mountains are hot and forbidding in the summer, but can be lush with wildflowers in the early spring. The bluebonnets that grow there are different from the ones in central Texas, and are taller. This painting was done entirely with palette knives and is very textured.

Texas Tranquility

This is a scene from my friends Pat and Frank's place near Stephenville. These are Pat's horses: Coco, Clue, and Penny. This was done with palette knives.

Johnny's Spot

This was my first painting to use the "smooth surface" technique I learned from Dalhart Windberg. Johnny was a longhorn bull who lived next door to my friends Pat and Frank near Stephenville. Johnny was a gentle animal and would let you approach and pet him.

Utopia, Texas

I've never been to Utopia, Texas, but it looks like a nice place to visit or live. The Sabinal River runs through the canyon in Uvalde County.

Prickly Pears

This is one of my first palette knife paintings. Getting the paint to come off the edge of the knife to do the thorns and the shadows of the thorns took a little practice.

Upland Jewels

When my wife and I lived in El Paso, I spent a lot of time driving through and exploring Big Bend National Park. This rugged, beautiful land has many mountain trails and scenic overlooks. It is home to many species of cacti, including yucca and prickly pears. The desert in bloom is a sight to behold; the air is filled with the fragrant perfume of cacti and other plants as they call for pollinators to come and enjoy their tasty treats.

– Other Landscapes and Seascapes –

Sea Reflections

A limited palette painting using red, black, yellow, and white.

Doodlebug and Friends

If you're ever in Jacksonville, Florida, be sure to eat at Singleton's Seafood Shack. That's where I found Doodlebug, along with a lot of her friends.

Catch of the Day

I enjoy doing miniature paintings. I can do one in a few days instead of several weeks. This and all the other 5 x 5 paintings were donated to the Arts Center of the Ozarks for their annual benefit auction.

Point Lobos, 1579

Point Lobos is located south of Carmel-by-the-Sea and Monterrey, and is considered by many to be the crown jewel of California state parks. This view is from Headland Cove, and adjoining it is one of the richest marine habitats in the world. This scene depicts Sir Francis Drake and his ship The Golden Hind sailing up the coast in 1579. Legend has it that Drake sailed north of what is now San Francisco and put ashore to claim the land for Queen Elizabeth. On the stern of the ship is a female deer, which the English call a hind.

Pride of Yosemite

El Capitan, part of Half Dome, and Bridalveil Fall are shown from across the Merced River. Those rocks in the river are slippery, I learned.

Moraga Morning

Moraga is a California town in the Bay Area, east of Oakland. It was first inhabited by the Saklan Indians. After being settled by Spanish explorers, the area became the Moraga Ranch, and cattle were raised during the nineteenth century. Now with a population of around 18,000, most of the remnants of this earlier world are gone. This painting was based on a photo I took from a residential neighborhood lined with houses and cars. I painted the scene as it might have looked when it was still a ranch, but I did add St. Mary's College, which moved to Moraga in 1928.

Lizard on a Rock

Based on a composite of photos taken in the Superstition Mountains in Arizona. Four Peaks mountain range can be seen in the distant background. And there is a lizard on a rock.

Sacred Place

Monument Valley is an awe-inspiring landscape and is home to the Navajo people. I added a hogan, which faces east to catch the morning sun.

Still Lifes

Fruit of the Earth

I found these shaggy mane mushrooms growing in Ontario. They are delicious sautéed with butter and served over brown rice. I left these alone so they can spread their spores in peace.

Endless Forms

Plants, fungi, acorns, and a six-spotted tiger beetle. The title is from the last sentence in Darwin's *On the Origin of Species*: "There is a grandeur in this view of life, with its several powers, having originally breathed into a few forms or into one; and that, whilst this planet has gone cycling on according to the fixed law of gravity, from so simple a beginning endless forms most beautiful and most wonderful have been, and are being, evolved."

The Why of White

A limited palette painting.

The Odd Couple

My first attempt to paint a glass.

Zuni Memory

The Museum of Native American History is in Bentonville, Arkansas. The curator allowed me to photograph a 1000-year-old Zuni pot. The pot had been glued together from hundreds of shards. I painted it as though it were new and in use in a pueblo all those centuries ago. I wonder whose hand made the pot and painted the beautiful designs.

Bass Reeves, Headin' Out (20 x 30)

Bass Reeves was born a slave in Arkansas in 1838. When he was eight years old, he and his family were moved to Texas. When a teenager, he got into an altercation with his master and ran away to the Indian Territory in what is now Oklahoma. He lived with the Indians, learned their culture and language, and learned to shoot a gun. After emancipation, he moved to Fort Smith, Arkansas, and became a U.S. Deputy Marshall working for "Hanging Judge" Parker. Reeves was big, strong, and ambidextrous. He was an exceptional marksman and could shoot with either hand. He would disguise himself and drive his wagon to the Indian Territory, bringing back outlaws that hid there by the wagonload. He became one of the most feared and respected Deputy Marshalls at that time. He built a home in nearby Van Buren and married his sweetheart Nellie Jennie, his first wife. They had several sons before Nellie died at an early age. He became an officer in the Muskogee Police Department before his retirement and death in 1910.

We Can, We Will (18 x 24)

The title of this painting is the motto of the Ninth Cavalry Regiment of the U.S. Army. Formed in 1866, the regiment became known as the Buffalo Soldiers. The regiment provided protection to settlers during the westward expansion into Texas and other states and saw combat in the Indian and Spanish—American wars.

Lone Star Heritage (12 x 24)

The written history of Texas begins with the arrival of the Spanish Conquistadors, who arrived in the early 1500s. But Texas had already been occupied by many different peoples for as many as 15,000 years before that. During these millennia, cultures came and went, but the land and the wildlife remained about the same until the European settlers wiped out the buffalo, cleared the forests, and built cities. The little mouse hides beneath the buffalo skull, waiting to finish its meal of corn.

Awaiting His Hands (18 x 12)

This commissioned painting shows my friend's grandfather's antique Bedrock hand plane along with other period tools. I like working with cherry wood myself, and it was fun painting the cherry shavings. Painting the various steel and brass surfaces was challenging and rewarding.

Made in U.S.A. (18 x 24)

This painting is a tribute to my mentor, Dalhart Windberg. The photo in the painting is Dal in 1950 with his brand-new Indian Chief motorcycle. The motorcycle parts are Indian parts from a 1930s bike. Dal's favorite drink is Dr. Pepper, and a friend loaned me his old Dr. Pepper can to include in the composition. The oil can belongs to Dal, and he was kind enough to let me borrow it. The patch on the wall was loaned to me by a stranger who used to ride Indian motorcycles. Doing all the stitching on the patch was challenging, as was the Pegasus and lettering on the oil can. The title of the painting is on the bottom of the oil can. This painting won the "Best Oil Painting" award in a five-state regional art show hosted by the Arts Center of the Ozarks. I showed this painting to Dal at one of his workshops. The other students really liked the painting and asked Dal, "Does Johnny get a 10?" Dal smiled and said, "Nobody gets a 10." He's right. There is always room for improvement, and no painting is perfect.

About the Artist

Panoramic vistas of ancient Ozark mountains lit by the last rays of the setting sun. Texas hills and valleys covered in the brilliant hues of autumn. Crystal waters flowing through time-eroded landscapes older than Man. These scenes of the natural world are the inspiration for the realistic and intricate oil paintings of Johnny Bowen.

Bowen's award-winning and widely collected paintings reflect his own sense of wonder and awe of nature, and his techniques follow in the footsteps of the great American landscape artists of the nineteenth century. Initially self-taught, Bowen soon made contact with respected Texas artist Dalhart Windberg and became a student of his in 2000. Bowen's representational realism is influenced by Windberg as well as by the nineteenth-century artists of the Hudson River School. "My painting heroes include Durand, Church, Moran, and Bierstadt, and I aspire to create the same feeling of the sublime wonder of the natural world as did these great artists."

Bowen grew up in Fort Worth, Texas, and developed a life-long friendship with a boy who lived down the street, Mike Baldwin. "Mike and I spent a lot of time exploring the creeks and fields around Fort Worth, looking at protozoans through Mike's microscope, and viewing the heavens through the telescope Mike and his Dad built. Mike was very influential in sparking my interest in science."

Bowen met his future wife, Peggy, when they were students at the University of Texas, Soon after marriage and graduation, they moved to Arkansas and have lived on Sugar Mountain south of Fayetteville for over forty years. "After traveling around the country, we decided that northwest Arkansas was as pretty a place as we had seen, and we moved here as soon as we could," Bowen recalls. They have two children.

www.bowengallery.com

About the Poet

Michael Baldwin is a native of Fort Worth, Texas, and may be descended from the Lakota mystic warrior Crazy Horse. He'll be glad to tell you that tale over a couple of beers. Baldwin holds a BA in political science and master's degrees in library science and public administration.

Now retired from a career as a library administrator and professor of American government, Baldwin's poetry has been published extensively in literary journals and anthologies. His poetry was featured on the national radio program *The Romantic Hours* and has twice been nominated for the Pushcart Prize.

He was awarded the Violet Newton Prize, 2000, for the poem "Lovedrunk Lunar Eclipse"; won the Eakin Manuscript award, 2011 for his poetry book, *Scapes*; and won the Morris Memorial Chapbook Award, 2012, for *Counting Backward From Infinity*. His book of Texas poetry, *Lone Star Heart* (Lamar University Press, 2016) vied for the Texas Institute of Letters Poetry Book Award. His book *The Quantum Uncertainty of Love* (Shanti Arts Press, 2019) was a National Book Award nominee.

Baldwin has also published: a mystery thriller, *Murder Music*; four collections of science fiction short stories: *Passing Strange, Surpassing Strange, More Than Passing Strange,* and *Beyond Passing Strange*; a children's science/adventure book, *Space Cat*; a book of humorous Texas ranch stories, *Chronicles of Frank*; and a book of flash plays, *A Few Bricks Shy of a Chevrolet.*

Baldwin resides in Benbrook, Texas, with his wife, Helen. They are active with several community charities, coach a local high school tennis team, and help nurture their two wonderful grandsons.

www.jmbaldwin.com
bit.ly/AmazonBaldwin

Shanti Arts

Nature ▪ Art ▪ Spirit

Please visit us online
to browse our entire book catalog,
including poetry collections and fiction,
books on travel, nature, healing, art,
photography, and more.

Also take a look at our highly regarded art
and literary journal, *Still Point Arts Quarterly*,
which may be downloaded for free.

www.shantiarts.com

www.ingramcontent.com/pod-product-compliance
Lightning Source LLC
LaVergne TN
LVHW060620110826
845147LV00019B/1055

* 9 7 8 1 9 5 6 0 5 6 0 5 1 *